Healing Our SOULS

WALKING WITH THE GOD WHO GATHERS OUR TEARS AND MENDS OUR HEARTS

by

PAMELA MARJORIE

Published under the pen name *Pamela Marjorie*

Royal Kingdom Publishing

Scripture quotations are taken from the Holy Bible, King James Version (KJV), unless otherwise noted.

This book is a work of personal reflection, faith-based insight, and lived experience. It is intended for inspirational and educational purposes only and is not a substitute for professional medical, psychological, psychiatric, or pastoral counseling. The author is not a licensed medical or mental health professional. Readers are encouraged to seek guidance from qualified professionals regarding their own physical, emotional, mental, or spiritual well-being.

Any references to healing reflect the author's personal journey and spiritual understanding and may not represent the experiences or needs of every reader.

Some names and identifying details have been changed to protect the privacy of individuals. Any resemblance to actual persons, living or deceased, is coincidental.

Printed in the United States of America First Edition

To purchase copies or contact the author:

Healing Our Souls Ministries LLC

1445 Woodmont Lane NW, Suite 456
Atlanta, GA 30318

Tel: 7707670183

Email: Support@HealingOurSouls.com

Website: HealingOurSouls.com

ISBN: 979-8-234-06003-7

Royal Kingdom
PUBLISHING

DEDICATION

This book is dedicated to my Lord and Savior Jesus Christ, to God my Heavenly Father, and to my Comforter, the Holy Spirit. I also dedicate it to myself for not quitting in spite of the challenges, and to my beloved children, Jourdan and Olivia, who have been my greatest teachers in love and faith, and whose lives continue to shape the woman God has called me to be.

This journey has not been easy, but I trust God that we will have the victory in the end. I could not have chosen two more special people to walk through this life with.

ACKNOWLEDGEMENTS

My oldest sister, Joan, has always been like a mother to me. She loves me unconditionally and was the first person in my life with whom I felt completely safe. I could tell her anything without fear of judgment or concern that my words would one day be used against me. She rarely, if ever, became angry or annoyed with me, and her steadiness became a refuge throughout my life.

When I became a mother, her love extended seamlessly to my children. She moved states twice to help care for them while I worked, offering her presence, devotion, and time without hesitation. Though she had no children of her own, she became a second mother to mine, and for that I am forever grateful. To this day, I honor her each Mother's Day for the role she has played in my children's lives and in mine.

My deepest gratitude also goes to my best friend, Belinda McClenton, whom I have known for over twentyfive years. Belinda saw things in me long before I could see them in myself. She has loved me and my children unconditionally and never misses an opportunity to remind us of that love. Where I once searched for acceptance in relationships, it was always present with Belinda. She has been constant and faithful, the one God sent to stand with me through thick and thin. Her presence in my life has been a living reminder of what true friendship, loyalty, and Godgiven love look like. Though we are not sisters by birth, we are forever joined by the heart and united as soul sisters.

I would also like to acknowledge my siblings, Angela, Donovan, Marcia, Stacey, and Paul, as well as Laura, who has been like a sister to me, each of whom has walked alongside me at different points in my life. I am thankful for the shared history, for the support offered in various seasons, and for the ways God continues to work through family, even when relationships are complex. I also extend my love to my eldest niece Kristin and her husband Joshua, who opened their home to me when I needed it most. I am deeply thankful for my many nieces and nephews. They are too numerous to name here, but each one is dearly loved.

I would be remiss not to include my "adopted" sons and daughters who lovingly call me Ms. Pam or Mama Pam, many of whom are friends of Jourdan and Olivia, as well as the family members and dear friends who have walked this journey with me. There are too many to name, but you know who you are. Your love, support, and encouragement have carried me more than you will ever know.

A special acknowledgment to the following people who showed extraordinary love and support to me and my family when we needed it most: Auntie Jenny, Vangie, the Flavins, Ms. Eva, Ms. Toni, DaQuan, Julian, Ms. Stephanie, Mason, Ms. Danielle, and Coach Brian. Your generosity and care have meant more than words can express, and I will always be grateful for each of you.

FOREWORD

By Belinda McClenton

Over twentyfive years ago, I met this beautiful woman in a bridal shop, wearing the most gorgeous wedding gown. Her beauty captivated the room, and I simply had to tell her how stunning she looked. At the time, I had no idea that moment would mark the beginning of a lifelong friendship and sisterhood. The love I have for her is unwavering.

Over the years, our friendship has blossomed. We attended each other's weddings, walked through divorces side by side, and watched our children grow as life threw its fair share of curveballs our way. Through it all, Pam has remained a woman grounded in faith, trust, and love. Her most cherished role is being a mother, one of her greatest accomplishments, as she poured unconditional love into her children from the time they were babies through adulthood.

The resilience she shows in every situation and the compassion she lives by have helped shape me into the woman I am today. Her spirit is gentle and kind, yet strong, even through life's ups and downs. She is always willing to step in, help you navigate your situation, and find a way forward. Pam has seen me at my worst and still stood beside me, helping me move through darkness until I could see the light again. My sister and best friend helped me believe in life, love, family, and myself. She is truly a blessing to me and to everyone who knows her.

No matter what season of life I was in, Pam never looked down on me. She never pitied me or judged me. Instead, she taught me how to get back up, dust myself off, and find a way forward, even when I thought it was impossible.

Pam's life and journey will show you that God can do amazing things if you simply believe. I have witnessed her walk through profound challenges as a parent and endure deep personal hardship, yet she chose prayer, trusted God, and allowed herself to move through a healing process with courage and faith.

This book will open your eyes, mind, and heart to what healing through God truly looks like. It will show you how a woman who faced adversity allowed it to become a doorway rather than a dead end. Like so many of us, Pam understands trauma and generational patterns that can impact our lives. Her story is one of love, healing, and restoration through Christ.

The woman behind this book is smart, resilient, beautiful, and profoundly loved. She is truly one of God's greatest blessings.

I invite you to step into these pages with an open heart, and may Pam's journey encourage you to trust God with your own story and believe that healing and restoration are still possible for you.

PREFACE

I will tell my life story with the same rawness with which it unfolded. The reality is that I have forgiven myself, the people who hurt me, and the people I have hurt. I am either healed from many of these wounds, or I am still actively working through them.

Let me preface the telling of my story by saying this: it is not my intention to deliberately hurt or offend anyone. I am here to share my truth, and I will handle it as gently as possible without changing or sugarcoating what happened. I can only tell this story from my perspective.

This is why God wanted me to write this book. My story is your story. If you can see even a small part of yourself in these pages, and if you are willing to do the work, you too can be freed from the shackles of the mind, will, and emotions. Healing is a process that unfolds over time, often revealing only what we are ready to see in that moment. It requires awareness, honesty, and a willingness to partner with God in the work He is doing within us. God gently reveals the hurting and broken places of our hearts, not to shame us, but to heal us. "He heals the brokenhearted and binds up their wounds" (Psalm 147:3).

This book was written from my faith in God and my belief in the saving grace found through Jesus Christ. My prayer is that these pages would not only bring healing to wounded places but also lead you into a deeper relationship with God, where true restoration begins. If as you read, you sense that something has been missing in your life, or you have felt a quiet pull toward God but were unsure how to begin, I want you to know that you are not alone. God is near, and He is reaching for you even now. If you feel ready to give your life to Him, or to return to Him with an open heart, you will find a simple but powerful prayer of salvation later in this book. When you come to it, read it slowly and say it with sincerity. God meets us exactly where we are, and He honors a willing heart.

This book is not meant to rush or overwhelm you. You do not need to understand or apply everything at once. If one chapter speaks to you, stay there. Sit with it. Pray through it. Work through it for as long as you need until you experience peace and freedom. God is faithful to meet us exactly where we are, and He will complete the work He has begun in you (Philippians 1:6).

My hope is that as you read, you begin to recognize patterns, emotions, and beliefs that may have shaped your life in ways you did not previously understand. As awareness comes, you can take the steps outlined here, or elsewhere as the Lord leads, to bring healing to what He brings to the surface. Awareness is often the doorway to freedom, for "you shall know the truth, and the truth shall make you free" (John 8:32).

TABLE OF CONTENTS

HEALING OUR SOULS . HEALING OUR SOULS . HEALING OUR SOULS . HEALING OUR SOULS .

INTRODUCTION

"And the Lord answered me, Write the vision, and make it plain upon tables, that he may run that readeth it."

Habakkuk 2:2

INTRODUCTION

"For I know the thoughts that I think toward you, saith the LORD, thoughts of peace, and not of evil, to give you an expected end." — Jeremiah 29:11

On Easter Sunday in 2025, I stood in line outside 2819 Church with my daughter Olivia, waiting to enter service. As I stood there, aware that my healing journey was far from complete, I heard God speak to my spirit and tell me to write a book about my journey. As I often do when I sense God leading me, I immediately said yes in my heart.

I was excited and told Olivia right away. She responded with a familiar, unimpressed look. I had shared many inspired ideas with her over the years. Some I started, others I did not. What remained consistent was that I was not a finisher.

Making a decision has never been hard for me. Following through has been another story. Inspiration alone is not enough. It takes discipline and perseverance to see something through. I have struggled with lack of confidence, perfectionism, and a deep fear of getting things wrong. With each passing year, it became harder to believe in myself, and doubt took deep root. Although I was a devoted mother and a loyal friend who showed up for others without hesitation, when it came to myself, especially creative or personal work, I often stalled. This was an area of my life that had not yet been healed.

I already had notes from the healing work I had done, more than enough to begin writing, yet I convinced myself to wait. At the time, I believed I needed my Kingdom Mate before telling the full story. After all, everyone loves a happy ending. We are conditioned to expect the princess to get the prince, or in my case, the queen to get the king. Without realizing it, I had absorbed the idea that my story was incomplete unless it ended that way. So, I stepped back from writing and put the book on hold.

A few months later, I was on an entrepreneurship call and feeling discouraged. There were close to two hundred people on the call, and many of them were writing books. The enemy started ministering to me. Yes, the enemy ministers too. That seed of doubt began to spring up again.

Why should I write this book? Everybody is writing a book. How am I going to be different? What can I say that someone else has not already said? I went to sleep that night feeling dejected, turning those thoughts over in my mind.

When I woke up the next morning, I got on my knees and prayed. I was honest with God about how I was feeling. I heard Him speak in my mind, which is the primary way God communicates with me. I know it is God because there is a sense of peace in what is being said. I heard, "There is something I want you to say, exactly the way you say it, that nobody else has said. There are people who will identify with what you are saying. These are the people I have chosen to learn and grow from the seeds you have sown."

Then I heard, "Your life is not your own. You were bought with a price" (1 Corinthians 6:19–20). While this passage speaks directly to sexual purity, its meaning extends beyond that context. It is a reminder that our lives belong to God, that we are not selfmade or selfdirected, and that we are called to live in obedience to Him. In other words, Pam, get over yourself. This is not about you. This is about Me. I created you for a purpose, and I expect you to fulfill that purpose. *Obedience is better than sacrifice.*

With that, I began writing God's book, the book He commanded me to write. What I did not yet understand was the journey God would take me on, how His love for me and for you would continue to unfold through this process, or how much healing still lay ahead. Healing Our Souls was a name given to me over twentyfive years ago, a few years after I first committed my life to the Lord. I was not yet rooted in the Word of God and did not know what to do with that assignment, and in time, I fell away. But God, in His faithfulness, brought me back to finish what He began in me. As Scripture reminds us, "And I am certain that God, who began the good work within you, will continue His work until it is finally finished on the day when Christ Jesus returns" (Philippians 1:6, New Living Translation). Now, you have a frontrow seat to that assignment coming full circle, as He continues the work of healing my soul, and in turn, ours.

EPIGRAPH

“I said, Lord, be merciful unto me: heal my soul, for I have sinned against thee.” — Psalm 41:4

Healing

A restorative process through which God brings wholeness to the soul, mind, and heart over time.

Soul

The nonphysical essence of a person, encompassing the mind, will, and emotions.

“He sent His word, and healed them, and delivered them from their destructions.” — Psalm 107:20

CHAPTER 1

Fear thou not; for I am with thee: be not dismayed; for I am thy God: I will strengthen thee; yea, I will help thee; yea, I will uphold thee with the right hand of my righteousness.

Isaiah 41:10

CHAPTER 1

HOW GOD USES OUR BACKGROUND IN OUR CALLING

One of the most overlooked truths in the story of Moses, in the book of Exodus, is that God used the very parts of his background that seemed confusing, painful, or out of place. Moses was born a Hebrew but raised in the palace of the very empire that oppressed his people. To some, it looked like an identity contradiction, but it was actually divine preparation. Everything Moses thought disqualified him was exactly what God intended to use.

His Egyptian education, his exposure to leadership, even his years spent as an outsider in Midian all became the foundation of his calling. Nothing in God is wasted. In the same way, the experiences we often hide or question - our wounds, our detours, our rejected places, and the seasons where we felt "out of place" - all become the soil where purpose grows. God weaves every chapter of our story into the assignment He gives us.

GOD USES EVERY SEASON

What gives me comfort in Moses's story is not just where he came from, but when God called him. Moses wasn't a young man full of strength and confidence when God set him apart to deliver His people; he was eighty years old. Eight decades of complicated identity, painful experiences, wandering, self-doubt, and unfulfilled potential. Yet when Moses told God he couldn't speak well enough for the assignment, God answered him with words that healed something deep inside of me too: "Who made man's mouth? ... I will be with your mouth and teach you what to say." God didn't choose Moses because he was eloquent. He chose him because he was available. And the years Moses thought were lost were actually the years God was preparing him.

But God's use of Moses doesn't mean only late calling. God uses early ones too. In the book of 2 Chronicles we learn that King Hezekiah began to reign at twenty-five years old, and early in his rule he led the people of Judah in restoring the Lord's temple and refocusing the nation on faithful worship (see 2 Chronicles 29:1-11 and 2 Kings 18:1-7). Hezekiah's zeal so early in life reminds us that God can call us into meaningful, purpose-driven work in whatever season we are currently in. God's timing is perfect. You are never too young or too old for His purposes.

In my case, it showed me that it is never too late to be used by God, and that the story He allowed to unfold for me, the painful parts, the waiting seasons, the experiences that shaped me, will resonate with the women who are in the same place I was. God will put His words in my mouth just as He did for Moses, and just as He will do for you. God uses our background, even the painful parts, in our calling.

JOURNAL PROMPTS

1. What season of life do I feel like I am in right now? Do I feel like I am healing, preparing, transitioning, being called forward, rediscovering myself, or simply uncertain?

2. How can I partner with God in this season instead of resisting it?

3. What is in my hand that God can use today? (My story, my gifts, my pain, my experience, my wisdom, my testimony?)

4. What part of my past have I viewed as wasted or too painful, and how might God be preparing to use that very area for healing, purpose, or impact?

Prayer for Purpose and Preparation

Father,

I thank You that nothing in my life has been wasted. Just as You prepared Moses through every season, his identity, his pain, his wandering, and even his insecurities, I believe You are preparing me.

Teach me to see my story through Your eyes. Remind me that it is never too late, and that You are the God who calls, equips, and speaks through willing vessels.

Use what is in my hand. Use what is in my heart. Heal what is still tender and make my voice an instrument of Your grace.

I surrender my past, my experiences, and my gifts to You. Put Your words in my mouth and guide me into the purpose You designed for me before the foundation of the world.

In Jesus' Name. Amen.

HOW IT STARTED

The Broken Engagement

What began this most recent healing journey was a broken engagement. I was only four weeks back into church and reconnecting with the things of God when my friend Loreyna came to visit me for her birthday. While we were out together, I noticed several couples around us. The women looked vibrant and well put together, while the men appeared disengaged and neglectful of themselves. In that moment, something settled in my spirit. I knew I did not want that kind of partnership.

When we returned to my home, before going to bed, I prayed earnestly and sincerely, asking God to bring me a man whose heart matched my own. Around three in the morning, I had a vivid dream. In the dream, I heard the name of a childhood friend, and I was told he was my husband. His first and last name were spoken not once, but twice. "This is the third time I am coming to you. In the mouth of two or three witnesses every word shall be established" (2 Corinthians 13:1).

Given this, I was convinced I had heard from God. I had not spoken to David in over thirty years. I had moved several times and had no idea if he still lived in our hometown. I could not sleep, so by six that morning I searched for him on

Facebook. I found him. There were no photos of a wife or girlfriend, which to me felt like a green light to move forward.

I sent David a simple message saying hello and asking how he was doing. Two hours later, he responded with his phone number. I was on my way to church and could not respond right away, but later that afternoon we spoke. We reminisced about childhood memories, and it felt comforting to reconnect with someone who knew me before adulthood, someone other than my siblings.

As it turned out, David lived less than three hours away, in the same state I had moved to just three months earlier. He had been living there for years. Again, this felt like confirmation. I quickly began evaluating whether he could be a suitable partner. When he asked why I had reached out after all those years, I shared that I had dreamt about him and felt prompted to contact him. I did not tell David I believed he was my husband. I did not want to overwhelm or frighten him.

Shortly after we began talking, David asked me to dinner. I asked directly whether he was inviting me as a friend or on a date, explaining that my expectations were different for each.

David hesitated, then lightly admitted it was a date. Our date was set for two weeks later. He was a gentleman and picked me up, and we had already agreed he would stay in town at a hotel and attend church with me the following morning. I was genuinely excited. When David arrived, I stepped into the car and immediately felt like something was off. When I'm first around a person I tend to sheepishly watch them determining if they are safe. It takes some time for my nervous system to settle down and feel safe. I am scanning constantly for danger. My five senses are on alert for anything that could be out of the ordinary. I thought I smelled alcohol, but didn't know if I was overthinking, so I let myself focus on the music playing softly and the easy banter between us as we drove.

Earlier, on two separate phone calls, I had noticed subtle signs that made me cautious. His speech had seemed a little slurred. Having grown up around alcohol, I had learned to notice these things. When I gently asked about it, David assured me it was nothing more than a few drinks while watching football.

During dinner, he ordered two strong drinks. It seemed he was pacing himself, holding back to stay in control. To anyone else, it might have gone unnoticed, but I felt a subtle warm rush over my body, that familiar feeling of unease. I questioned myself again. Was I projecting? Was this fear? Or was I picking up on something I needed to be aware of? Ignoring these feelings, I chose to focus on the ease of our conversation instead. I had a glass of wine myself, relaxed into the moment, and enjoyed laughing and reminiscing together. I began to soften and give the connection a chance.

Over the following weeks, we talked regularly, and I grew more comfortable. David was attentive, generous, and kind. He was willing to do almost anything for me, something I had never experienced before. I told myself this must be the man God had for me, especially since we shared a sense of history.

I was cautious about committing until I could observe how he interacted with family and what kind of father he was. Less than a month later, my daughter and I spent the holiday with David and his family, which gave me that opportunity.

Soon after, we entered a committed relationship. I explained that I did not intend to have sex before marriage, yet I made choices that compromised that boundary, such as spending late nights alone together. Four months into dating, we became engaged. Not long after, I began noticing David's drinking pattern more clearly. I started feeling like it was more than I was comfortable with.

I did not want him to change for me, and I knew this was not a situation that would make me happy, so I called off the engagement, and we parted as friends. I also realized that we were not aligned in several important areas, one of them being how much drinking was comfortable in a relationship, and another our spiritual beliefs. I also take responsibility for moving the relationship forward too quickly, thinking I had heard from God. I was left confused. Why would God put me in the one situation he knew I was not meant to be in? How had I drawn this pattern into my life again? I believed I had healed beyond this and was finally ready for a healthy relationship.

Maybe I had not heard from God, and that confusion led me deeper. What I discovered was humbling. I was not as healed as I believed. There were unresolved beliefs, unexamined patterns, and spiritual strongholds still operating in my life, including ways I had tried to control situations or silently go along with things that were not in God's will. As painful as this experience was, I am grateful for it. It forced me to stop skimming the surface and finally begin the deeper work God was calling me to do.

JOURNAL PROMPTS

1. What patterns do you see emerging in this story?
2. What patterns have you noticed repeating in your own relationships or decisions?

DISCERNMENT REQUIRES MATURITY

This experience made me aware of how far I still was in my walk with God. I had returned to church, and that prayer was sincere, but I was still learning how to pray effectively, how to listen, and how to remain consistent. It had been years since I had walked steadily with God, and my foundation was fragile.

When we lack spiritual maturity, we may hear something that sounds good and move too quickly. Familiarity can feel like confirmation, and desire can be mistaken for discernment. True discernment develops over time and is tested. I have heard it said that when God wants to bless you, He sends a person, and when the enemy wants to destroy you, he also sends a person.

God began growing me quickly in our relationship.

As each month passed, my faith deepened. I attended church regularly and began fasting and praying more. I also came to understand something important. While David believed in God and referred to God as Father in prayer, he did not see Jesus as Savior. He believed Jesus was only a prophet. He was always polite and appreciative when I shared Jesus with him, but he had not made a personal decision to follow Him.

We were not aligned on this critical truth. As of this writing, we remain friends, and I continue to share Jesus with him. Not because I hope he will be my husband, but because I care deeply about where people spend eternity. When you know the truth, you do not gatekeep it; you have a responsibility to share it with love.

Looking back, I can see that when I reconnected with David, I was not as surrendered to God or as spiritually clear as I thought I was. My choices were shaped by unresolved wounds and long-standing patterns I had not yet examined. God did not cause the situation, but He allowed it to reveal what was still unhealed in me. In a very real sense, I got what I prayed for, a relationship that reflected my (unhealed) heart. This breakup did not end something God had ordained. It exposed what God wanted to heal.

Through the loss of the engagement, God began showing me more of Himself and more of myself. He was not only revealing the condition of our relationship. He was revealing the condition of my inner and outer life and what still needed attention. I had not fully consecrated myself to God, walking with one foot in the world and the other in the church. That was the moment I understood that the issue was not simply who I chose. It was what I carried into the choice.

MOVING FORWARD

To understand why this relationship unfolded the way it did, I had to look beyond the present and into the past. The patterns did not begin with David, and they did not end with him. They were shaped long before, through family dynamics, learned behaviors, and beliefs I absorbed without realizing it. Some of what I carried came through my family. Some came through culture. Some came through coping mechanisms that once helped me survive but later clouded my judgment. Before I could choose differently, I had to see what I was bringing with me.

HEALING OUR SOULS . HEALING OUR SOULS . HEALING OUR SOULS . HEALING OUR SOULS .

CHAPTER 2

Before I formed thee in the belly I knew thee; and before thou camest forth out of the womb I sanctified thee, and I ordained thee a prophet unto the nations.

Jeremiah 1:5

CHAPTER 2

THE STORY I INHERITED

MY MOTHER'S STORY

My mother was born to Esther Jane and George Dacres in Jamaica, West Indies. She grew up with two brothers and a sister. She was a smart woman. She finished high school, which was no small thing, and worked for the Jamaica Omnibus Service. Later, she worked as a secretary for a political party, where she would eventually meet my father.

Before any of us, there was another child.

My mother's firstborn was Lorna Patricia. Lorna died at three months old from whooping cough. My mother described her as a sweet and beautiful baby. That loss lived quietly in our family, but it was always there. We do not know how old my mother was when she had Lorna, but we know she was twenty-three when she gave birth to Joan. The rest of us followed in quick succession, as if life did not give her much time to grieve before demanding more from her.

My mother was engaged to Joan's father when she became pregnant with Joan. They married while Joan was still in her womb. The relationship was unstable from the beginning. Joan's father was deeply jealous, and their connection was marked by cycles of separation and reconciliation. During one of those breaks, my mother became pregnant again, this time with Angela.

Angela was born five years after Joan. When she was only a few months old, a man my mother had previously been involved with took her, claiming he was her father. The police were called, and Angela was returned safely. The immediate danger passed, but the fear and sense of instability stayed with our family.

Over the next several years, our family grew quickly. Nineteen months after Angela, my brother Donovan was born, followed sixteen months later by my sister Marcia, who shares the same father as Donovan. Fourteen months after Marcia, I came into the world, completing our close-knit group of siblings.

At some point, my mother shared with us that she wanted a partner. She wanted help. She wanted companionship. But each time she reached for love, she ended up carrying more responsibility alone. With every new man came another child, another layer of pressure, another reason to keep going even when she was exhausted.

My mother gave far more than she received in her relationships. That pattern did not begin with her, and it did not end with her. Her ability to choose healthy partners had been deeply wounded. My sisters and I inherited the consequences of that wound, before we could understand its meaning. This was not just personal pain. It was a bloodline issue, passed quietly from one generation to the next.

On the surface, my grandparents' marriage appeared stable. They stayed together for many years, until death separated them. But even there, there was brokenness. My grandfather had an affair and fathered a daughter, Seiko, who is the same age as my sister Joan. Fidelity and safety were already compromised in the foundation my mother came from.

Years later, my mother told me that she had been molested by her uncle. I was in my early twenties when she shared this with me. I did not think to ask how old she had been. At the time, I did not know about trauma or generational wounds, or how deeply those early violations could shape the choices she made later, and the environment her children would grow up in.

As if that were not enough, her brother later stole the money she had saved for years to move us from Jamaica to England. That betrayal completely changed her life. It would be a decade or more before she could save enough to relocate, and by then she had four more children. When she finally left Jamaica, it was not for England after all, it was for the United States.

In 1969, my mother left Jamaica to make a better life for the five children she left behind. We stayed in our own home. Her best friend, who lived next door, cooked for us, washed for us, and checked in daily. My oldest sister, Joan, was thirteen and became responsible far beyond her years. I was four when my mother left. To me, it felt like she vanished. I did not have the words for it then, but I felt abandoned.

Although this was not the truth, that feeling settled into my little body early and stayed with me until this healing journey. This is how early experiences form what some call limiting beliefs, quietly running in the background like an operating system, shaping how we think, feel, and respond without us even realizing it. My little mind could not understand why my mother was gone. I could not see that she had left temporarily to make a better life for me and my siblings. In my body, it felt like rejection. It felt like abandonment. That became my truth, even though it was a lie.

When my mother arrived in America, she worked as a domestic, taking care of the entire household by cooking, cleaning, washing, and looking after their children. From there, she secured full-time work at a psychiatric hospital and part-time work at an adult group home. She became a Licensed Practical Nurse and worked relentlessly. In just two years, she saved enough money to build a house and bring all five of us to the United States.

Her sacrifice was enormous. Her strength was unquestionable. I am forever grateful to my mother for what she did to give us opportunity and stability. I don't know that we ever told her that enough. And I don't know that she ever fully rested from what it cost her to survive.

LEAVING ON A JET PLANE

I was six years old when we moved to America. I remember getting on the Air Jamaica plane, which seemed enormous to me. The song *I'm Leaving on a Jet Plane* was playing. I remember being served food, and everything felt exciting, like we were leaving our old life behind to begin a new adventure. I could not have imagined then how hard that journey would be.

Although my mother and Joan's father were no longer married, he still migrated to America with us. We settled in

Long Island, New York, staying with one of my mother's friends while our new house was being built. It took two months after we arrived for the house to be finished. During that time, we often walked the one mile from Ms. Ann's house to check on its progress. I remember those walks, the anticipation, and the belief that something better was waiting for us.

My mother and Joan's father had a volatile relationship. His jealousy was constant, and she seemed to provoke it. They could not make it work, and eventually he left to live with his sister in Brooklyn, New York. He would later return and cause more pain.

At some point, my mother flew to England to marry a man named George, someone she knew from her days in Jamaica. This was not a marriage based on love. It was an arrangement so he could become an American citizen. I remember seeing the wedding pictures. My mother wore silver because this was not her first wedding. George wore a black suit, a crisp white shirt, and thick black glasses. There was a picture of them feeding each other cake. My mother looked happy. She played her part well. George looked stern, which I would later learn was accurate.

While George waited for his immigration paperwork, my mother lived her best life. She had a boyfriend named Leslie, who we called Les. Les lived with us until the day George was scheduled to arrive in the United States. Les always did the driving, and that day he drove us to the airport to pick George up. I went along with my sister Marcia because I loved my mother and wanted to be near her and going to the airport felt like an adventure.

Les knew about George. I don't know if George knew about Les. That night, my mother hosted a welcome party for George and invited all her friends, including Les. Everything seemed fine until it wasn't. After the guests left and the children were in bed, including me and Marcia in a downstairs bedroom, raised voices woke us. The sounds from upstairs made it clear that things were getting physical.

We ran upstairs with our other siblings to protect our mother. Marcia jumped on George's back to stop him from touching our mother and hit him with a glass, which broke in her hand and cut her. I was pulling on George's leg, while my older siblings tried to separate them. I was seven years old. Marcia was eight. Joan, only sixteen, took control. She had Donovan carry our mother out to the car so we could get away.

We followed and piled into the car and drove to Les's family's house. There were so many of us that we slept on the floor. Between the hardness of the floor and the fear in my body, I did not sleep at all. I lay awake longing for morning. Even though George did not know where Les lived, my seven-year-old mind was convinced he would find us and kill all of us. What I needed that night was simple. I needed someone to hold me and tell me we were safe. I did not get that, not that night or on the other nights when violence happened at home. As a result, I developed a nervous stomach.

I was nine years old when Joan's father molested me. There were several occasions when he had me sit on his lap and eventually touched my breasts. It stopped after a separate incident, when he locked my mother in the bathroom and threatened to kill her. Joan removed the door handle with a butter knife and stood there with an ice pick in her hand, threatening to kill him if he harmed our mother. She made him leave that day, and he went to live with his sister in Brooklyn.

I later told my mother what he had done to me. She had little to say. I think it reminded her of what had happened to her and was too painful for her to face.

We continued to see him on some weekends because my mother had him doing projects around the house. He built an outdoor patio and a barbecue pit. They had a friendship, but they were not romantically involved again. He never touched me again, and no one ever confronted him about anything he had done. Silence was part of our family pattern. To ease tensions, my mother would take us out for ice cream instead of discussing what happened. Terrible things occurred, and we never talked about them.

When I was in my twenties, he fell off a ladder while working and suffered a serious brain injury. We were told he was not expected to recover. I planned to go to the hospital, even though he was barely conscious. I wanted to free both of us from the past by offering forgiveness and release. By the time I arrived, he had passed, and they would not let me see him.

At his funeral, I sat in my seat and said the words I needed to say silently. A small measure of relief came, but I could feel that there was still much healing left to do. This moment showed me that forgiveness is not about the other person. It is about freeing your own heart, even when the circumstances are beyond your control.

On the outside, my mother was tough as nails. I nicknamed her the Dragon Lady. While I loved her dearly, I was also very afraid of her. Raising five children while working constantly would harden anyone, and at times she worked three jobs. She demanded strict obedience and ran a tight household.

One day, while still in elementary school, Marcia and I disobeyed her and went to our friend Bonita's house, just two doors down. My mother forgot something at home, turned around, and caught us. She told us to go home and said she would deal with us later. We knew what that meant.

When she came home from work, she wasted no time. Marcia and I were naked in the bathtub and hit with an extension cord and a piece of an old garden hose wrapped together. In many families, this was considered discipline and was likely a carryover from slavery. After the beating, she made us kneel at the foot of her bed on smooth stones, sometimes for what felt like hours. Eventually, in the wee hours of the night, she let us go to sleep. We climbed into bed with her and fell asleep without anger, without resentment, only relief.

Yet there was another side to my mother, a softer, more compassionate side.

She was always willing to help others. When we rented rooms in our home, she would tell the tenants, "We're all one big happy family." My mother was a people pleaser in ways that often worked against her. Some tenants went months without paying rent, and she would not put them out until the situation became unbearable. We would get frustrated with her for being so kind to other people when it felt like it came at our expense. Many of her friends came to her for advice or help, and she rarely turned anyone away. That tendency to overextend herself was something me, Angela, and Joan would later recognize in ourselves.

There always seemed to be a party in those early years. There was always something to celebrate. If we were not hosting one, we were attending one at a friend's house. The adults played loud music, danced, played cards, and drank. The children were not left out. We were in the same rooms and were allowed to drink as well. The belief was that learning to drink at home would prevent us from learning the wrong way in the streets.

Most of the time there was laughter. Sometimes there was too much alcohol. Fights would break out. There were moments when men fought over my mother, and we had to step in to protect her. She thrived on male attention. Jealousy made her feel loved.

Looking back, I believe the seed of self-destruction was planted when her uncle took away her right to her own body. This is not uncommon. Many people who are abused or molested grow up carrying shame, self-hate, and a desperate search for love. I grew up inside the consequences of that wound.

THE GIFTS SHE PASSED DOWN

By the time my mother reached her mid-forties, she was finished with men and relationships. In her earlier years, she could drink a sailor under the table. As time went on, alcohol became less social and more necessary. She was less able to hold her liquor, though no one outside our family would have known she had a problem. She never missed a day of work because of drinking. The bills were always paid. There was always a roof over our heads. From the outside, everything looked intact.

My mother was fifty when I left home to attend college in New York City. When I came home on weekends, I would hug my mother and tell her I loved her. Before that, we did not say those words to each other. In our family, affection was assumed, not spoken.

They called me "Baby Pam," partly because I was the youngest, but also because I was sensitive. I think it was that sensitive spirit that compelled me to express love more openly. Even now, I am usually the first to tell my siblings that I love them. They say it back, though it often sounds a little awkward. I know they love me.

I don't know if this is a Jamaican thing, but we grew up teasing one another instead of encouraging each other. My sister Joan was called "four eyes." My sister Marcia, who is darker-skinned, was called "blackie." I was called Baby Pam in a taunting way and "big lip." I hated both of those nicknames. Words mattered to me, even when no one else seemed to notice.

Despite that, growing up with four siblings was also a lot of fun. There were always games to play and roles to assign. We created our own version of *Family Feud*, complete with a host. During Christmas breaks, we would stay up all night playing Monopoly, Bingo, Pokeno, and card games, laughing and driving my mother crazy. My brother Donovan was always the banker, and somehow he always ended up winning Monopoly.

Like most kids, we loved snow days. Donovan would walk less than a mile through deep snow to the 7-Eleven to buy us snacks, though he never did it for free. He charged us a premium. Those memories still carry warmth.

By the time my mother retired at fifty-five, alcohol had become a dependency. She grew tired of the lifestyle and the drama. The parties stopped. The friends stopped coming by. The men stopped too. She turned inward and focused on her home and her family. Her life became quiet.

As the years passed, it felt as though my mother slowly lost her will to live. She often said she wanted to live long enough to see me graduate from high school. I was thirty-two years old and a new mother when she made her transition. Years of drinking had enlarged her heart, and she died from a heart attack at sixty-five. We were with her until the very end, and she waited until we stepped out of the room before she passed. I had the sacred privilege of praying with her, reciting the Twenty-Third Psalm, and releasing her on her journey. We told her she no longer had to hold on for us, and that we would be okay.

One day I called my mother, distraught because two of my sisters were not speaking to me. My mother said, "Pamela, you are one of the nicest people I know. Ignore them." That was twenty-seven years ago, just a few short weeks before my mother would transition. I held onto those words. She also sarcastically called me Mother Teresa, because as a baby Christian I was always trying to share my faith with others. I suppose I have not changed all that much. My mother had a great sense of humor.

My mother showed me what it looks like to keep going when stopping is not an option. She believed deeply in hard work and in doing things to the best of your ability. She taught me that responsibility does not wait for healing, and that rest is often postponed in order to provide. From her, I learned how to work diligently, how to give my best even when I was tired, and how to endure seasons that are difficult.

She did not live an easy life, and she did not leave this world untouched by what she endured. Still, she raised five children on her own, kept us housed, fed, and educated, and made a way where there often seemed to be none. Even when she was weary, even when she was wounded, she did not abandon her duty. Along the way, she taught us gratitude, kindness, respect for others, and the importance of good manners.

I honor her for that. I honor her resilience, her determination, and her refusal to give up. I also honor the cost of that strength, and the parts of her that never had room to rest.

Another thing I noticed in my mother, and have only recently begun to acknowledge and accept in myself, is a kind of knowing. I once shared something with my sister Joan that I sensed was going to happen, and she said, "You have the same thing as Manan," which is what we called my mother. My mother often seemed to know things about people, sometimes through dreams, such as when someone was pregnant.

This is the inheritance I received from my mother. Not perfection, but perseverance. Not ease, but endurance. And from that foundation, I am learning how to live differently, with more gentleness than she was ever allowed.

MY FATHER'S STORY

I was born in Jamaica, West Indies, to unmarried parents. My mother was thirty-two and my father was twenty-four when I was born. My parents separated when my mother was five months pregnant with me.

Years later, when I was grown, my father shared what happened. He told me he had been drinking heavily and became consumed with jealousy. My parents were arguing over Marcia and Donovan's father, a man my mother was still in contact with and, in my father's eyes, giving too much attention. In a heated moment, my mother put my father out of the house and threw his clothes outside.

He was so intoxicated that, standing outside, he believed he had the strength to lift the house off the ground, like Samson in the Bible. When he failed, he simply went on his way.

My mother did not contact him when I was born. At that time in Jamaica, communication meant seeing someone in person, sending a letter, or passing a message through someone else. Eventually, my father saw her at a bus stop and asked whether she had given birth to a boy or a girl. She did not answer him there, but instead invited him to come to the house and see for himself.

My father had desperately wanted a girl, and I was his heart's desire. He fell in love with me instantly. Although he was not present in my life on a daily basis, my oldest sister later told me that he visited often and was kind to all of my mother's children.

My father also told me that he tried to reunite with my mother, but she was not open to it.

I do not have as many stories to share about my father because I did not grow up with him. What I do know is that shortly after I was born, my father gave his life to the Lord. He told me he had a radical conversion experience and that he wrestled in the spirit with the devil for his salvation. While this was happening, those watching in the church saw him thrashing on the ground.

He attended church regularly and was a deacon in his church. Yet despite this powerful spiritual experience, his personal life remained complicated. He went on to have several children out of wedlock and was married two or three times. My father had eight other children with six different women. I am the oldest of his children and do not know all of my siblings.

He was a generous man, but his giving in relationships was often unbalanced. Many of his wives and the mothers of his children took advantage of him financially and emotionally. Over time, he earned a reputation and was given the nickname "Born to Lose," or "Borney" for short.

As I shared earlier, I left Jamaica when I was six years old. While living in the United States, I had only brief communication with my father. One reason was the pressure he placed on me, as his oldest child, to send money and clothes back to Jamaica for siblings I had never met. He began asking this of me when I was just fifteen. Although I was working, I resented it because I was still a child myself. He did not ask what I needed, only what I could send. I felt unimportant. I wanted to be his daughter, not a provider.

I returned to Jamaica in my mid-twenties and met two of my brothers, who were only a few years younger than I was. Over time, I again lost contact with my father as I became busy building my own life. We did not reconnect until I was thirty-five and preparing to get married.

Around that same time, I received a phone call from a young woman who said she was my sister, Stacey, a sister I did not even know I had. She explained that she had gotten my number from our father. I was skeptical at first and assumed she might want something from me. Instead, she simply wanted to know her big sister, the one she had heard so much about.

Her timing could not have been better. I invited her to the wedding, and we flew my father in, since I had not seen him in more than ten years.

My father did not walk me down the aisle. My brother Donovan did. That meant more to me than I can express. I did not have a consistent male presence growing up, and Donovan showed up for me in steady and practical ways. It felt right for him to have that honor. Later that evening, my father gave one of the most powerful speeches of the night, even quoting William Shakespeare. I was proud of him.

After that, my father and I developed a very close relationship. For many years he helped care for Jourdan and Olivia while I worked. He loved being a grandfather and was wonderful with my children. They adored him. Although he continued to live in Jamaica, he spent many summers with us and joined us on family vacations.

He also filled in gaps about his relationship with my mother and about my birth, restoring pieces of my story. At times he shared stories about the spirit world, including one in which he believed a ghost connected to Obeah, or witchcraft, chased him through the house and caused him to crawl under furniture to escape. He was not afraid of the spirit world.

We often heard him praying before bed at night and again early in the morning before leaving his bedroom. He prayed in his native language and in tongues. The children later imitated him because he would often end a sentence in tongues with "bam bam," as if he were calling down fire from heaven. He left a legacy of prayer and spiritual blessing that I now understand I can draw from.

In his seventies, my father found the love of his life. She was almost forty years younger than him, and they married in 2017. She cared for him faithfully until his passing in 2020. I am grateful he experienced love and companionship in his later years.

Stacey and I have continued to build a strong sister relationship since the day we met at my wedding in 2000. After my father passed, I also met my brother Paul, who is twenty years younger than me. We have established a meaningful relationship that I treasure.

WHERE DO I BELONG?

I am my mother's youngest child and my father's oldest. I was the bridge between two families, the only child in common to both worlds. That reality shaped some of my identity.

In my mother's home, I was the baby. I was seen as sensitive. In my father's family, I was the oldest, and because I lived in the United States while the others remained in Jamaica, there was an assumption that I was financially secure. There was an expectation that I could help.

The truth was very different. I was working hard to take care of myself and later to raise my own children. I was not established. I was building.

Being the youngest in one family and the oldest in another created confusion inside of me. In one place, I felt misunderstood. In another, I felt overburdened. There was also an unspoken tension that can come when families are divided across parents. When you are the bridge, there can be quiet questions of loyalty. Loving one side can feel, at times, like distancing yourself from the other. That tension can shape your sense of belonging in ways you do not know until later.

I learned to adjust depending on where I was, but I did not always feel known in either space.

Some of my siblings on my father's side and I never built a real relationship. We did not grow up together or share daily life, and over the years neither of us made consistent efforts to change that. Distance became normal.

From time to time, I would hear from them. The conversations rarely began with genuine interest in how I was doing or how my family was doing. They often moved quickly toward a request for money.

That pattern hurt more than I expected. I wanted connection. I wanted conversation. I wanted to feel like a sister, not a resource.

Eventually, I deleted Facebook Messenger, which had become the main way they contacted me. The random requests for help without relationship were painful. Many people who migrate to more developed countries carry this burden of expectation from family back home. You want to help, but it is not always easy to know when to give and when to say no without feeling guilty.

This is one reason I value my relationship with Stacey and Paul so deeply. Our connection is built on mutual care and concern for each other and our families. There is no transaction. There is relationship.

I have always questioned where I belonged, where I fit in. I know that I was loved by those closest to me, yet it did not stop me from feeling unseen in both worlds.

JOURNAL PROMPTS

1. Looking at your family history, what patterns do you notice around sibling relationships, marriage, commitment, or parenting?
2. Do any of those same patterns show up in your own life or relationships? If so, how?
3. Pray and ask God what parts of your story He may be inviting you to heal or rewrite.
4. What positive legacy did your parents or grandparents leave you that you can draw from?

CHILDREN OUTSIDE OF MARRIAGE

When I share my mother's story and my father's story, one detail becomes impossible to ignore. Both of them had several children outside of marriage. My parents were not anomalies. They were products of a culture shaped by generations of disruption.

In Jamaica and in many other formerly colonized and developing countries, marriage was not historically the foundation of family life. This was not because people did not value love or commitment. It was because the conditions required for stable covenant had been repeatedly stripped away.

During slavery, Black men and women were not allowed to marry. Families formed, but they were never protected. Parents and children could be separated without warning. There was no legal or social covering for the family unit. Love existed, but permanence did not. This created a deep imprint that echoed long after slavery ended.

After emancipation, many were technically free but economically trapped. Land, education, and financial opportunity were scarce. Marriage became associated with economic stability rather than covenantal unity. Men often felt unable to provide in a way they believed marriage required, so relationships remained informal. Children were born and loved, but frequently without the structure of a committed marriage.

Over generations, this became normalized. People did what they had seen. They formed families the only way they knew how. My parents were not intentionally rejecting marriage. They were repeating patterns that had been modeled all around them. What was common became acceptable. What was acceptable became generational.

The Bible tells us that God establishes families by design. From the beginning, marriage was meant to be a covenant of covering, unity, and continuity. A man shall leave his father and mother and be joined to his wife, and the two shall become one flesh (Genesis 2:24). This design was never meant to restrict, but to protect.

When that design is interrupted across generations, children feel the impact. Many grow up without seeing covenant modeled. Father absence or emotional distance becomes familiar. Instability feels normal. Children often adapt by becoming self-sufficient early, emotionally guarded, or overly responsible. These adaptations help them survive, but they can quietly shape the choices they make as adults.

Scripture speaks to this reality when it says the iniquities of the fathers are visited upon future generations (Exodus 20:5). This is not a statement of condemnation. It is a recognition of how patterns travel through families. At the same time, Scripture promises that God shows mercy to thousands of generations of those who love Him (Exodus 20:6). Awareness opens the door to healing.

The absence of marriage in my family line did not mean an absence of love. It meant an absence of structure, consistency, and covenant. And when covenant is missing, children often carry a longing for stability into adulthood, sometimes without understanding where that ache began.

Naming this truth matters. It allows us to separate personal shame from generational trauma. It helps us understand why these patterns are so deeply rooted, especially in cultures like Jamaica where this was widespread and normalized. And it reminds us that what was learned can be unlearned.

God is a restorer of foundations. He rebuilds what history disrupted (Isaiah 58:12). In Christ, we are not bound to repeat what we inherited. A new pattern can begin with awareness, healing, and alignment with His design. The story does not end where it began (2 Corinthians 5:17).

In today's generation, marriage is no longer always seen as the ultimate goal. Our modern society has accepted non-covenant relationships as the norm. Many people are dating for companionship, fun, or convenience rather than for a lifelong commitment. When marriages are few and children are born outside of covenant, the fabric of society is affected, and families often carry the consequences. The institution of marriage has faced challenges from the very beginning, going back to the garden of Eden, when the serpent introduced division and discord.

If this pattern of marriagelessness or disrupted family life has been part of your family, know that God offers restoration. You do not have to repeat what has been passed down. Healing, forgiveness, and the rebuilding of covenant relationships can begin today. If this resonates with you, say this prayer with your whole heart. Repeat it as often as you need. Pray until you see the changes you desire.

PRAYER FOR GENERATIONAL HEALING, FORGIVENESS, AND RESTORATION

Father God,

I come before You with humility and truth. I acknowledge the broken patterns in my family line. I acknowledge the absence of covenant marriages, the wounds of separation, and the generational impact of disrupted families.

I repent, on behalf of my bloodline, for every way marriage was dishonored, misunderstood, or inaccessible. I repent not with shame, but with understanding. I ask You to cleanse what was carried forward unknowingly and to heal what was passed down unintentionally (Daniel 9:4–6).

I choose to forgive my parents for what they could not give. I forgive my ancestors for what they did not know. And I forgive anyone who has harmed us and the systems that stripped families of protection, dignity, and covenant. I release resentment, anger, and judgment into Your hands. You said in Your Word that if Your people who are called by Your name will humble themselves and pray, and seek Your face, and turn from their wicked ways, then You will hear them from heaven and forgive their sins and will heal their land (2 Chronicles 7:14).

In the Name of Jesus Christ, I renounce every demonic attachment tied to marriagelessness, abandonment, fatherlessness, instability, fear of commitment, sexual brokenness, and orphanhood. I break agreement with every lie that says marriage covenant is unsafe, love does not last, or family cannot be trusted (John 8:36).

Jesus, You are the restorer of all things. I ask You to heal the residue of slavery, separation, and loss that still lingers in the souls of Your people. Restore what was stolen. Rebuild what was broken. Reestablish covenant where it was disrupted (Joel 2:25).

I receive Your design for family, love, and legacy. I declare that a new pattern begins with me. By Your grace, future generations will know stability, covenant, and healing. What was fractured will be made whole. What was lost will be redeemed (Isaiah 61:3).

I seal this prayer in the authority of Jesus Christ, who redeems bloodlines and makes all things new.

In Jesus' Name. Amen.

HEALING OUR SOULS · HEALING OUR SOULS · HEALING OUR SOULS · HEALING OUR SOULS ·

CHAPTER 3

And he said unto them, full well ye reject the commandment of God, that ye may keep your own tradition.

Mark 7:9

CHAPTER 3

GENERATIONAL PATTERS AND FAMILY WOUNDS

Many of the traditions woven into Jamaican life trace back to Africa. Enslaved Africans carried their customs, beliefs, and spiritual practices with them to the Caribbean, and over generations these traditions blended with Christianity and Caribbean culture. As a child, I didn't understand the history, I only felt the impact of these customs on my tender little soul.

Some of my earliest and most unsettling memories came from how death was honored in Jamaica. When someone passed away, the body was not taken to a funeral home as is common today. Instead, the deceased was laid out in the family's parlor or living room until burial. As an adult, I can appreciate that this practice was meant to show love and respect. But as a three- or four-year-old girl, it was terrifying to walk into a room and see a body lying there for days while life carried on around it.

This period of mourning and celebration is known as "Nine Nights." Its roots lie in the people of West Africa, who believed that a person's spirit takes nine nights to journey from this world to the next. Families and neighbors gathered each night to sing, pray, share stories, and ensure the spirit traveled safely. On the ninth night—the final farewell—some families would prepare a symbolic meal for the departed or turn the mattress where the person last slept so the spirit would not return.

Over time, Nine Nights has evolved; what was once a solemn communal ritual often looks more like a lively party. But its origins are deeply spiritual and rooted in community, meant to honor the dead and support the living.

For me, however, witnessing a body in the home stirred a fear of death that felt far bigger than my small body could hold. Everyone else seemed calm, even joyful, but my little heart was overwhelmed.

As if that weren't enough for a young child to process, the Christmas season brought another cultural tradition that frightened countless other children: Jonkonnu, pronounced *John-Canoe*. Jonkonnu is a masquerade festival rooted in African resistance to slavery, an artistic defiance wrapped in music, satire, and dance. Colorful characters parade through the streets with drums pounding and rhythms rising, a celebration of survival and identity.

But to a child, the spectacle feels more like a nightmare. Many performers wear exaggerated masks or costumes meant to mock colonial power or represent spirits. Characters like Pitchy Patchy, Cow Head, and the Devil often had distorted features, pale faces, or frightening expressions, very similar in effect to the Halloween costumes Americans wear today but amplified by the thunder of drums and the excitement of the crowd.

Then came the towering stilt walkers who move 8 to 10 feet skillfully in the air. In African tradition they are spiritual protectors and guardians who can see danger from above. Adults viewed them with admiration. Children, however, were often chased or teased by dancers and masqueraders, all in the name of fun. For me, it only deepened my fear.

What the adults saw as cultural joy and entertainment, some children experience as chaos, noise, and terror, with no understanding of the deep African heritage behind these traditions.

Illustration of costumes at Junkanoo festival

OBEAH AND THE FEAR THAT FOLLOWED

In Jamaica, what many people refer to as witchcraft is often called Obeah. The term traces back to West Africa and became known throughout the Caribbean during the era of the transatlantic slave trade, long before Jamaica became an independent nation. Colonial authorities first outlawed Obeah in the eighteenth century after enslaved people used spiritual symbols and practices to strengthen resistance during an uprising. Over the next century, additional laws were introduced to suppress it.

One such law, passed at the end of the nineteenth century, remains in place today. It makes it illegal to claim the use of supernatural or occult powers to frighten, manipulate, or harm another person. While the law is rarely enforced in modern times, its presence reflects how seriously these practices were once feared and controlled.

Because Obeah has long existed in secrecy, there are no reliable statistics showing how many people practice it today. Cultural historians and journalists have noted that it continues to surface in certain communities and conversations, particularly in rural areas or in informal settings. More often than not, it remains hidden, whispered about, or stigmatized rather than openly acknowledged.

In recent years, there has been renewed public discussion about whether these old laws should be repealed or revised. Some argue they are relics of colonial fear and control, while others express concern about the spiritual and social consequences of normalizing practices rooted in spirit invocation.

Is this becoming normalized in Jamaica? I could not find a clear percentage to show how many people actively practice Obeah today. What I do know is that when fear takes root in the heart, it does not need statistics to feel real. What terrified us in those moments shaped how we understood the spiritual world long before we ever learned about the God who protects, redeems, and restores.

Jamaica was founded with Christianity woven into its national identity, and for generations many pastors and prophets have called the nation to remain anchored in God. When a devastating Category 5 hurricane struck the island in late October 2025 with unprecedented force, many believers viewed it as more than a natural disaster. With catastrophic winds, widespread flooding, loss of life, and billions in damage, it became one of the most destructive storms the nation had ever experienced. For some, it served as a sobering reminder and a call for spiritual clarity, a warning against straddling competing spiritual worlds and an invitation to return fully to God.

For many of us who grew up there, Obeah was not just folklore or rumor. It was a lived fear. Before I left Jamaica at six years old, I witnessed something that marked me deeply. The man many people feared was De Laurence. He was known in our community for casting powerful spells. His name alone was enough to silence conversations.

Our neighbor and family friend, Ms. Toomer, had a sister who owed someone money and did not pay it back. Because Ms. Toomer's sister was pregnant, the person who was owed the money chose not to harm her directly. Instead, they turned to Obeah and directed the punishment toward her daughter, Ms. Toomer's niece, a little girl around twelve years old.

My siblings and I witnessed rocks and spit flying through the air toward this child. The rocks struck her stomach, and she doubled over in pain as they fell to the ground. They were smooth beach rocks. We were nowhere near the beach. There was no logical explanation for what we saw. That moment lodged fear deep inside me and shaped how I understood the spiritual world.

What followed was not just fear of darkness or spirits, but fear of God Himself. I became afraid to fully surrender. I worried that if I truly let go, my eyes would be opened and I would see into the spirit realm and be overwhelmed with terror. Even the idea of seeing angels or Jesus frightened me, not because I did not love God, but because my earliest exposure to the unseen world had been rooted in fear, not protection.

Looking back, I believe this fear stifled whatever spiritual gift God had placed inside me. The enemy is strategic. He loves to steal our gifts early, especially when we are children, by attaching fear to what was meant to be sacred. What God intended for discernment, intimacy, and authority was distorted into terror and retreat. Healing, for me, meant unlearning fear and relearning who God truly is.

MY CULTURE MADE ME DO IT

Some of you will read the previous section and feel offended by what I have said about Africa, Jamaica, and Caribbean culture. I understand that reaction. Culture is deeply personal. It carries memory, belonging, and identity. At the same time, many of us come from cultures that include the worship of other gods and the honoring of idols. Scripture is clear that no idol is aligned with the God of the Bible. It is either devotion to Him alone or participation in what opposes Him. When we continue the idolatrous and witchcraft practices of our forefathers, we can unknowingly remain in sin and rebellion against God. These unexamined traditions can become open doors that allow the enemy to continue wreaking havoc in our lives.

Dan Crain, in his book *Christ Over Culture*, speaks about the need for a unified body of Christ that represents every race, nation, and tribe. His challenge is confronting and necessary. We must ask ourselves difficult questions. Are we willing to be separated from God for eternity because of our culture?

I know people who refuse to accept Jesus as the Messiah because of His ethnicity. Others struggle because He does not fit their image of what the Messiah should look like or who He should be. Scripture is clear about the facts. Jesus was Jewish. He was a descendant of David. His parents were Jewish. He was born in Bethlehem and raised in Nazareth. These details are not symbolic. They are historical.

This resistance is not new. Jesus Himself said, "A prophet is not without honor except in his hometown, among his relatives, and in his own household." What is familiar is often the hardest to receive. The people closest to Him struggled to see Him clearly because He did not arrive in the way they expected. They were waiting for a conquering king, not a humble Savior. Their expectations became a stumbling block.

In the same way, culture can blind us. When Jesus does not look the way we expect, speak the way we prefer, or affirm what we want to hold on to, we are tempted to reject Him altogether. The question then becomes painfully simple: Is the discomfort of surrendering our cultural version of God worth the cost of eternal separation from Him?

I admit that I once got caught up in the race conversation myself. I thank God that He used my son and my daughter to change my thinking. Truth has a way of confronting us through the people we love most. The devil is a liar, but God is patient, faithful, and relentless in His pursuit of our freedom.

PRAYER OF RENUNCIATION: RELEASING THE SPIRIT OF FEAR

Heavenly Father,

I come before You in humility and truth. I acknowledge that fear entered my life early, through experiences I did not understand and could not control. I renounce every spirit of fear, terror, intimidation, and false power that attached itself to my heart through culture, trauma, or inherited belief systems. I break agreement with fear in all its forms.

I declare Your truth over my life. You have not given me a spirit of fear, but of power, love, and a sound mind. I receive Your peace, Your protection, and Your authority. I ask You to cleanse my memory, restore what was stolen, and heal the places where fear distorted my view of You.

I choose to trust You fully. I release fear of the spiritual realm and receive the safety of Your presence. Where fear once silenced my gifts, I invite You to restore them. Where fear kept me distant, I draw near. I place my life, my spirit, and my future in Your hands, knowing that perfect love casts out fear.

In Jesus' Name. Amen.

JOURNAL PROMPT

Where did fear first enter your story, and what has it kept you from fully trusting or surrendering to God?

HEALING OUR SOULS · HEALING OUR SOULS · HEALING OUR SOULS · HEALING OUR SOULS ·

CHAPTER 4

Remember not the sins of my youth, nor my transgressions: according to thy mercy remember thou me for thy goodness' sake, O LORD.

Psalm 25:7

CHAPTER 4

THE WOUNDS WE CARRY

I started working at Citibank when I was just eighteen, a young girl trying to make her way in the world as a bank teller. By twenty-one, I was promoted to Customer Service Representative, feeling grown, proud, and stepping into life. That's when I met him. Curtis Matthews.

He worked for Brinks Security and delivered money to our branch on the Upper East Side of Manhattan. The first day I saw him walk in wearing that dark blue uniform, the gun on his hip, and that quiet confidence...our eyes locked. He was twenty-seven, just a few years older, but to me he seemed like a full-grown man. Mature. Steady. Gentle. Everything my twenty-one-year-old heart thought meant safety.

He asked me out not long after we started talking. Curtis drove a candy-apple-red Camaro, and like the movies, I believed I had stepped into my first real love story. We both lived in the Bronx. I stayed with my older sister, and he lived with his mother, helping her out. We spent most of our time at my place when we weren't out eating. And as would become the pattern for nearly three decades of my life, I fell in love fast. Too fast.

Just a few weeks into our relationship, everything shifted. Curtis told me another woman, Selena, was pregnant with his child. They had been together briefly before me. I was devastated. The kind of devastated that makes you feel like you can't breathe. When I asked why he didn't tell me sooner, his answer was simple and selfish: *he didn't want to ruin his chances* with me.

Not long after, I found out I was pregnant too.

When I told Curtis, he panicked. He insisted I couldn't have the baby because he already had one on the way. I can still remember the sound of his voice, frantic, pressured, and me, twenty-one and already carrying an impossible weight. I didn't want to bring a child into a situation that was already broken, so we made the decision to terminate the pregnancy. It remains one of the most difficult choices of my life. (I have since learned much more about abortion, and I hope to address the subject in another forum with compassion for the complexity many women and men face).

I was six weeks pregnant. He went with me. And though we were still "together" after that, something in our relationship, and something in me changed. I still loved him, but as Selena's pregnancy moved forward, we fell further apart. When she went into labor, he left me to go welcome his daughter into the world. I was heartbroken beyond words.

After the baby was born, Curtis's mother grew distant and didn't want me calling the house anymore. This was before cell phones, before easy communication. And then one day, while at a busy shopping area, I saw Curtis, Selena, and their newborn getting out of the car together. That image pierced me. I felt abandoned, replaced, rejected at the deepest level.

I spiraled so low I seriously wondered if life was even worth living. The pain was that deep.

For anyone reading this: *no one is worth you harming yourself.* No heartbreak, betrayal, or loss is the end of your story. You *will* love again. But love yourself first. Heal first. Pray first. And ask God to align you with a person who loves Him, cherishes you, and is truly called to your life. Anything else will only repeat the same cycle of pain.

AND MORE

That wasn't the only drama my twenty-one-year-old self went through with Curtis before his daughter was born. I had tried marijuana a few times before, but it never agreed with me. My nervous system was always too sensitive. What other people called "fun," my body interpreted as panic. But during those months with Curtis, wanting to be close to him and wanting to be "mature" enough to handle whatever he suggested, he introduced something that almost destroyed me.

He suggested trying a pill, something he said would "enhance intimacy." I didn't know what it was. I didn't recognize the dangers. And I certainly didn't understand what I was inviting into my body, my mind, and my spirit.

He put the pill in his mouth and then placed it into mine when he kissed me.

Within minutes, my entire body felt like it had been set on high alert. Every sensation became extreme. I was already on my period, feeling weak, and suddenly the pressure of a kiss was like smashing my lips against something hard. I could also feel every fiber of the sheets. In my altered state I imagined and felt my tear drops as ice cubes running down my face, every touch like it was scraping my skin. My nerves were firing like they were in overdrive.

Hours passed like that, terrified, overwhelmed, trapped in my own body and mind. Eventually, I begged him to take me to the hospital. They told me the drug had to wear off on its own and suggested drinking milk, which did nothing. It took nearly 24 hours for the sensations to settle, and for years afterward, well into my 30s, I would have flashbacks whenever I panicked or became overwhelmed.

I wouldn't understand until decades later that my nervous system wasn't just reacting to a drug, it was reacting to trauma that had been living in my body since childhood.

I understand now that some substances can open the door to experiences that are harmful and destabilizing, especially when a person already carries unresolved trauma. For me, the experience was not only physical. It disrupted something much deeper and left me feeling fragmented and unsafe inside my own body.

As part of my healing journey, I eventually brought that experience to God with honesty and accountability. I acknowledged that I had taken something I should not have and asked for His help in restoring what had been disrupted and dislodged by fear. That process helped me regain a sense of wholeness and stability, both emotionally and spiritually.

I also came to a clearer understanding of spiritual boundaries. I believe darkness is real, but I also learned that fear does not get the final word. Over time, I learned how to release the emotional and spiritual residue from the past, trusting God's authority rather than living under fear. At this stage of my life, I am intentional about what I allow access to my body, my mind, and my spirit.

LET'S TALK HONESTLY ABOUT SUBSTANCES

I'm not an advocate for drugs, none of them. Not marijuana. Not recreational anything. Not alcohol as a coping mechanism.

Culture normalizes these things, wraps them in "relaxation," "self-care," or "natural healing," but the truth is harder and less glamorous:

1. *No substance can heal what's hurting inside you.*
2. *If you need something to numb you, that's your body asking for healing not escape.*
3. *Just because something is legal doesn't mean it's safe or beneficial.*

People love to quote studies about wine being good for the heart until the truth came out that the benefits were from lifestyle, not wine. The same with marijuana: yes, certain medicinal uses exist, but smoking it, relying on it, or using it to cope can lead to mental, emotional, and physical harm.

Your nervous system matters. Your mind matters. Your spirit matters.

We live in a world where corporations profit from addiction, not healing. You must protect yourself. If you need a substance to feel good, calm down, fit in, or enjoy life, it's a signal:

Your soul is asking for care

Your body is asking for regulation

Your heart is asking to be seen

Your spirit is asking for God

WHEN IT HITS HOME

Addiction has touched my life in the deepest, most painful way a mother can experience.

My son, Jourdan, died at age 25 from fentanyl poisoning. Even writing those words, less than three years later, still feels unreal. The lessons I share here about spiritual warfare, the danger of normalized addiction, generational patterns, and emotional pain that gets numbed instead of healed, I learned most of them after his passing.

Had I known then what I know now, I sometimes wonder if things could have been different. But I no longer live in the torment of that question. I've placed it in God's hands and trust Him to use this experience for His purpose and for the healing of others.

Jourdan was kind, funny, and sensitive. My firstborn, loved deeply not just by me, but by his sister, father, family, and friends. He was taken too soon.

Understanding your family history is important. Patterns of pain, coping, and addiction can repeat across generations. When we turn to substances or behaviors to mask our pain, we risk opening doors that previous generations struggled to close. Even a single choice made in desperation or stress can plant seeds that grow over time. This is not about blame or shame. It is about awareness, protection, and making choices that may honor the life you have been given.

Your soul is asking for care, your body is asking for regulation, your heart is asking to be seen, and your spirit is asking for God. Recognizing this can help you break cycles that may have affected your family for years.

Behind every substance, every "just to ease my mind," every "I only do it socially," and every "it is not that serious," there is a family member or friend praying they will not get that call.

If sharing my story wakes up even one person, if it breaks denial, if it redirects someone back to God, or if it gives someone courage to seek help, then Jourdan's life continues to bear fruit. That is how I honor him.

JOURNAL PROMPTS

Take a moment, breathe, and be completely honest with yourself.

Not judged.

Not shamed.

Just honest.

So many people normalize drinking, smoking, pills, or "just having fun," but your soul will always speak the truth, even when culture does not.

Use these questions as a spiritual mirror. Let the Holy Spirit highlight what needs healing.

1. Have you found yourself drinking, smoking, or taking something to relax, "have fun," escape your thoughts, or quiet emotional pain?
2. Have you ever tried to slow down or stop and found you could not, even though you wanted to?
3. Do you have any family members who struggled with this issue?
4. Do you spend time with people who encourage, normalize, or pressure you toward substances? Pay attention: who you are around influences who you become.
5. Has your health, sleep, mental clarity, or peace been affected by substance use?
6. Have you ever made decisions under the influence that you regret, feel ashamed of, or wish you could take back?
7. Do you feel stuck, afraid to ask for help, or unsure where to begin?
8. Do you sense your soul is tired, overstimulated, or fragmented and know deep down that something has to change?

If you answered yes to any of these, this is not condemnation. The Holy Spirit is drawing you into deeper healing. You are not weak for needing help. You are brave for reaching out.

WHERE TO GET HELP: SPIRITUALLY AND PRACTICALLY

Healing often requires both spiritual guidance and practical support. One breaks spiritual bondage, and the other gives you practical tools to walk out your freedom.

Spiritual Help

- Your local church's deliverance or inner-healing ministry
- A trusted pastor or prayer team
- Christian counseling
- Prayer partners who walk in integrity and authority

Practical Help (U.S. Resources)

Sometimes you need someone to talk to immediately:

- **SAMHSA National Helpline (24/7): 1-800-662-HELP (4357)**

Free, confidential help for alcohol or drug recovery, counseling referrals, and support.

- **National Suicide & Crisis Lifeline: 988**

  If you ever feel overwhelmed, lost, or unsafe.

- Local recovery meetings (Alcoholics Anonymous (AA), Narcotics Anonymous (NA), Adult Children of Alcoholics (ACA or ACoA), Celebrate Recovery)

Deliverance Prayer for Freedom from Substances, Trauma, and Soul Fragmentation

Pray this out loud as often as you need to. Pray through until you get the breakthrough. Authority is released through your voice.

Father, in the Name of Jesus,

I come before You acknowledging every place where I have used substances to numb pain, escape reality, or fill a void that only You can heal. I repent for every door I opened knowingly or unknowingly through drugs, alcohol, or anything that altered my mind or invited spiritual interference. Father, forgive me and wash me clean with the blood of Jesus.

In the Name of Jesus, I renounce every spirit attached to substance use, addiction, bondage, escape, torment, anxiety, fear, confusion, fragmentation, and instability. I reject them and command them to leave me now and never to return. I declare that I am free, for Your Word says, "If the Son sets you free, you will be free indeed" (John 8:36).

Holy Spirit, fill every empty place. Restore every fragmented part of my soul. Bring back every piece of me that was shaken loose through trauma, substances, heartbreak, or fear. Integrate me back into wholeness according to Your Word, which promises, "He heals the brokenhearted and binds up their wounds" (Psalm 147:3).

Jesus, break every generational curse of addiction, escapism, emotional instability, and self-destruction in my bloodline. I declare that these patterns stop with me.

Fill me with Your peace, clarity, and strength. Teach me new ways to cope, rest, process, and heal. Surround me with the right people, the right support, and the right systems.

I declare in the mighty Name of Jesus that I am free.

In Jesus' Name. Amen.

FASTING FOR BREAKTHROUGH

If you feel spiritually stuck or need a deeper breakthrough, fasting is a powerful practice. Fasting exposes hidden bondages, breaks generational patterns, and positions you to hear God clearly.

One of the most impactful fasts I have encountered is Tiphani Montgomery's *Year of the Bride Fast (August 2025).* It focuses on breaking bloodline patterns, spiritual oppression, and reclaiming your God-given identity. The content is not limited to marriage or women; as a believer, you are the Bride of Christ. You can find her videos on YouTube by searching her name or the fast title. Please see the Resources section for additional fasting suggestions.

Fasting is not about starving yourself. It is about starving everything that has been starving you.

HEALING OUR SOULS · HEALING OUR SOULS · HEALING OUR SOULS · HEALING OUR SOULS ·

CHAPTER 5

That if thou shalt confess with thy mouth the Lord Jesus, and shalt believe in thine heart that God hath raised him from the dead, thou shalt be saved.

Romans 10:9

CHAPTER 5

FAITH AND SALVATION

My mother made us go to church when I was a pre-teen, and we were all water baptized, but we did not have a relationship with Jesus as I know Him today. That simply was not taught in our Baptist church. We sang a few hymns, listened to a nice sermon, which I did not pay attention to, and then went back home. It was a Sunday morning ritual.

My mother sang in the choir and over the years became very discouraged with the church. She said it was hypocritical. The deacons were sleeping with members and were known to enjoy a few hard drinks.

When I was about fifteen or sixteen, my sister Angela got saved in a charismatic church, and I began going with her. I had never seen a church like that before. They were operating in the gifts of the Spirit, and healing took place. Wheelchairs, braces, canes, and other devices hung from the rafters, meant to symbolize healing and what people no longer needed. I loved going to that church.

I do not remember an altar call or formally giving my life to Jesus. Maybe there was one and I was too timid to walk down the aisle. In those days, you did not pray the prayer of salvation in your seat like you do today. When my sister stopped going, I stopped too. I did not drive, so I had no way to get there on my own.

After graduating high school, I moved to New York City to attend college and ended up living in Brooklyn. One day, while walking down my block in Prospect Heights, I ran into a couple who worked at my job. I did not know they lived in the neighborhood. We started talking, and they invited me to church the next day. The church was in Connecticut, and I drove with them.

I felt the Spirit of God in that place and was radically saved. A few days later, I was filled with the Holy Spirit with the evidence of speaking in other tongues. I will never forget October 28, 1992, the day I was born again. I began making the drive from Brooklyn to Connecticut three times a week to attend church. Jamie and Ben were so kind and gifted me a Hebrew and Greek Key Study Bible that I still use today. A few months later, they moved to Connecticut to be closer to the church. I felt like I belonged there.

At the time I got saved, I was living with my boyfriend of three years. When I learned that this was against God's will, I asked him to move out. We broke up and remained distant friends. Eventually, I moved to Connecticut to be closer to the church.

CHURCH HURT

This church was filled mostly with young people between the ages of sixteen and thirty. It was small and felt like a family. Because of what I believed was my faithfulness, the pastor asked me to be on the Board of Directors. He explained that he needed to mentor me so I could pass the board interview

He took me out to dinner on a Friday night after church services. We talked about the board process, and then he began confiding in me. He started calling me at work and eventually told me that from the day I walked into the church, he knew he had married the wrong woman. I was shocked. He had never looked at me inappropriately. I was 27 and still too trusting, and he was in his early forties, married for more than ten years to a beautiful woman, with four children.

We were very devout in that church. If a skirt or dress was above the knee, we placed a cloth over our legs. He regularly preached that fornication was a sin against God. His nephew wanted to date me, and he would not allow it. I did not realize at the time that he had other intentions.

He kissed me, and although I kissed him back, deep down I knew this could not be the will of God. I was confused. Why would God put me in this position? Had I not been faithful enough? I did not idolize the pastor. I was respectful, honorable, loyal, and obedient. I was on fire for God. Why me?

I did not understand then that unresolved wounds can make a person vulnerable, even in church.

I passed the interview and became the only non-family member on the board. Being in the inner circle gave me a close-up view of what happened outside the pulpit. I was not pleased with what I saw and heard. People were not as kind as I thought they were, and my image of a perfect church began to shatter.

Between what I witnessed and the pastor's advances, I became deeply disillusioned and stopped attending church. The pastor often said that God did not speak directly to us, only through him. Eventually, I did not just leave the church. I slowly drifted away from God.

I felt abandoned, as if God had chosen the pastor over me. My obedience and love did not feel like enough. This mirrored how I felt about men in my life. My father was not present, and every father figure I trusted had betrayed me. I concluded that God would betray me too.

Church members began calling to ask why I was not attending. I could not tell them the truth, so they assumed I had fallen into sin. One day, the pastor's sister left a message on my answering machine. She said she understood what I was going through. I heard empathy and sadness in her voice, though I did not understand what she meant at the time. Later, I learned I was not the only woman this had happened to. I was fortunate that I left before it went beyond a kiss.

I had introduced my best college friend to the church. She and her boyfriend both gave their lives to the Lord and later married there. I was her maid of honor. I could not tell her what had happened either. I did not want to interfere with anyone's walk with God. I convinced myself that his behavior was a lapse in judgment and that I should not cause scandal. The scripture, "touch not my anointed," echoed in my mind, something he had often quoted.

My friend and her husband remained at the church for many years. I always felt judged rather than supported, and despite a few attempts to reconnect, the relationship was never the same.

When my Connecticut lease ended, I moved back to my old apartment in Brooklyn. I attended Brooklyn Tabernacle and was water baptized there. I was hesitant to join any ministry and kept people at a distance. I attended church, but my heart was guarded. Eventually, I drifted away again. I loved God, but I was afraid of church.

USE ME, LORD

During the three most devoted years of my walk with the Lord, I sang with all my heart, *"If You can use anything, Lord, You can use me."* I closely followed the healing ministry of Kathryn Kuhlman, who often spoke about the price one pays to be used by God. At that time, I was not married and did not have children. My life was simple. I had no idea how costly that prayer could be.

ENCOUNTERS WITH GOD

On Saturdays, we street witnessed, sharing the gospel and leading people in the prayer of salvation. One Saturday, my heart was overflowing with joy over what God was doing in the community. When I drove back to my condo in Brooklyn, I was distracted. I parked my car a few doors from my building, locked it, and went inside.

The next morning, I walked to my car to go to church and discovered it was gone. I was in disbelief. My car had been stolen. I called Jamie and Ben, and they gave me a ride to church. Once there, I was prayed for and encouraged not to worry.

When I returned home, I sat on my bed and cried out to God from the depths of my being. The glory of the Lord filled my bedroom. It looked like a light fog, the air charged with electricity, and a deep peace settled over me. If anyone had walked into that room, they would have felt the weight of God's presence. In that moment, I knew everything would be okay.

That night at eleven o'clock, I received a call from an unfamiliar number. They told me they had my car and would return it for a fee. I felt a boldness rise in me and told them all I could give was one hundred dollars. They immediately agreed.

They turned out to be two teenagers who lived a block away. I had left my key in the door, and they took the car for a joyride. They found my Bible in the car, looked at my registration, and called 411 to get my number. I could smell marijuana in the car. I spoke to them gently, prayed for them, encouraged them to stay out of trouble, and urged them to give their lives to the Lord. We all went on our way. That is the power of God.

On another occasion, after I had stopped attending church but was still living in Connecticut while waiting for my lease to end, I was brushing my teeth when I heard a voice as clearly as if someone had spoken into my ear. The Holy Spirit warned me that someone very close to me had made a decision that would directly impact my life. The message was brief, only a few words.

I am not at liberty to share the names or specific details, as it involved people I loved and a very sensitive situation. What I can say is that it was not something I could have known naturally, nor something I would have expected to be revealed to me.

Two weeks later, during a heated exchange, the truth came out exactly as the Holy Spirit had warned me. That moment confirmed to me that God speaks, protects, and sees what we cannot. Looking back, I now understand that the warning was not meant to shame anyone, but to guard my heart and redirect my steps. Shortly afterward, I made the decision to leave Connecticut and return to Brooklyn, trusting that God was leading me away from harm and toward healing.

PAY NOW OR PAY LATER

"I am the way, the truth, and the life. No one comes to the Father except through Me." — John 14:6

I want to pause from telling my story to share my faith, because this is the purpose of my story. We are in a spiritual battle for our souls, a battle between God and Satan (the devil). It is a battle between good and evil, and whether you believe it or not, you are in the middle of it. I cannot afford to be wrong about Jesus and salvation, because what is at stake is where my soul will spend eternity. I choose to follow the guidance of the Bible, the best-selling book of all time, historically accurate, with fulfilled prophecy and a unified message written over 1,500 years by 40 authors across three continents.

According to God's Word, if you have not accepted Jesus Christ as your Lord and Savior, you are not in God, and your name is not written in the Book of Life. Savior of what? Savior from eternal separation from God and from a literal place called hell.

God did not create hell for humans. Hell was created for Satan and the fallen angels who rebelled against God. Sin entered the world through that rebellion, first revealed in the deception of Eve. The serpent, representing Satan, promised Eve that eating from the tree of the knowledge of good and evil would make her like God. That original sin opened the door to humanity's separation from God. That same deception continues today.

Satan deceives people into thinking they can reach God apart from Jesus Christ, or that they are gods themselves. He diverts people through religion, fractured truth, and endless variations of belief systems. There are over 45,000 Christian denominations and more than 10,000 religions globally, many borrowing selectively from Scripture. At their core, there are only two forms of spiritual worship:

- Worship of the one true God, the God of Abraham, Isaac, and Jacob
- Worship of other gods or spiritual forces, whether openly acknowledged or subtly disguised.

Satan has further confused humanity with new doctrines, new books, and alternative ideas claiming truth. These texts often reference the Bible but redefine or diminish the authority and divinity of Jesus Christ. Jesus said, "I am the way, the truth, and the life. No one comes to the Father except through Me" (John 14:6). Why choose another path that diminishes His position? Truth does not need revision.

Sin, by definition, means missing the mark, by actions, thoughts, or omissions against the will of God. God is holy and cannot coexist with sin, which leads to spiritual death. But there is hope. That separation can be overcome through faith in Jesus Christ, who offers forgiveness, redemption, and restoration. Through Him, we are reconciled to God and rescued from eternal separation.

You have a choice. Surrender your will, pride, and self-rule to God now, making Jesus the Lord of your life and decisions, or pay later through eternal separation from God. Everything in the spiritual realm has a cost. The price is paid either now through obedience and faith, or later through judgment. There is no neutral ground.

SCRIPTURE REFERENCES

- John 14:6
- Genesis 3:1–6 (The Fall)
- Isaiah 14:12–15; Ezekiel 28:12–17 (Satan's rebellion)
- Matthew 25:41 (Hell created for the devil and his angels)
- Romans 3:23; Romans 6:23 (Sin and separation from God)
- Romans 5:12 (Sin entering through Adam)
- 2 Corinthians 11:14 (Satan disguises himself as an angel of light)
- Acts 4:12 (Salvation through Christ alone)

SATAN THE DECEIVER

Satan is a trickster. He is a liar and a deceiver, and he has one goal: to keep you separated from God.

He wants you to believe false doctrines—or no doctrine at all. Maybe you identify as an atheist and do not believe in God. Maybe you are agnostic and unsure what to believe. Either way, the truth remains the same: when you leave this physical body, you will stand before God.

There are no loopholes. There are no second chances. There are no philosophical arguments that will matter then.

If you have accepted Jesus Christ as your Lord and Savior with sincerity in your heart, and you live a life that seeks to honor God through repentance and submission rather than by performance or works, not willfully choosing sin day after day, you will be welcomed into your heavenly home.

This is not about perfection. This is about position.

When you stand before God having accepted Jesus as Lord, God does not see your sin. He sees His Son. Jesus took your sin upon Himself through His death, burial, and resurrection. But if you have rejected Jesus, you will stand before God alone, fully exposed, separated from Him for all eternity.

That separation is hell.

Hell is a real place. It is a place of darkness, completely devoid of the light of Christ. A place where there is no goodness, no peace, no relief. A place where pain exists without end. A place where you are confronted with every fear you avoided in this life. A place where the enemy mocks what you refused to surrender when you had the chance.

This is the single most important decision you will ever make.

Where you spend eternity.

Personally, I choose to err on the side of caution. I am not willing to pay the price of being wrong about Jesus.

I hate Satan. I hate what he has done to humanity. I hate how he deceives people and then blames God for the destruction he causes. He is not misunderstood. He is evil. And Jesus did not come to make us comfortable with darkness; He came to rescue us from it.

JESUS THE SAVIOR

If you have never accepted Jesus Christ as your Lord and Savior, or if you once walked with Him and know you need to rededicate your life, you can do that right here, right now.

Do not wait.

The Holy Spirit of God is tugging at your heart as you read this. That conviction is not fear, it is mercy. Do not ignore it.

Scripture tells us:

"If you confess with your mouth the Lord Jesus and believe in your heart that God has raised Him from the dead, you will be saved. For with the heart one believes unto righteousness, and with the mouth confession is made unto salvation."

— Romans 10:9–10

PRAYER OF SALVATION

Pray this Prayer of Salvation out loud with all your heart and all your soul:

Lord Jesus Christ,

I come before You today knowing that I am a sinner and that I cannot save myself.

I confess my sin to You, and I ask for Your forgiveness.

I believe that You are the Son of God,

that You died on the cross for my sins,

that You were buried,

and that You rose again on the third day in victory.

I turn away from my old life and surrender my life to You.

I ask You to be my Lord and my Savior.

Come into my heart.

Fill me with Your Holy Spirit.

Teach me to walk in Your truth and live a life that pleases God.

Thank You for saving me.

Thank You for the gift of eternal life.

From this day forward, I belong to You.

In Jesus' Name. Amen.

LET'S CELEBRATE

If you prayed that prayer with sincerity, welcome to eternity with God. Please email me at *support@healingoursouls.com* and let me know. I would love to celebrate with you. Understand this: salvation is not a one-time moment that ends here. It is the beginning of a daily walk with God.

Find a Bible-believing church where the Word of God is taught clearly and without compromise. Surround yourself with other believers. Read your Bible daily. If you do not own a Bible, buy one. God speaks through His Word.

In the next section, I offer guidance on how to discern what a healthy, biblically sound church looks like.

HOW TO DISCERN A BIBLE-BELIEVING CHURCH

This checklist is a guide, not a rulebook. Use this checklist prayerfully. No church is perfect, but a healthy church will align with the truth of God's Word.

- The Bible is taught as the inspired and authoritative Word of God, not selectively, not rewritten, and not overridden by tradition or opinion.
- Jesus Christ is clearly taught as fully God and fully man, not merely a teacher, prophet, or example.
- Salvation is taught as being by grace through faith in Jesus Christ alone, not by works, rituals, sacraments, or performance.

- The death, burial, and resurrection of Jesus are central to the message, not secondary or symbolic.
- Jesus is taught as the only mediator between God and man. No other person, saint, leader, or system is necessary for access to God.
- The Holy Spirit is acknowledged as God and active in the life of the believer, bringing conviction, guidance, comfort, and transformation.
- Repentance is taught as a turning away from sin and toward God, not ignored, softened, or replaced with self-help language.
- Sin is addressed honestly according to Scripture, without compromise, but also without condemnation.
- The gospel message remains consistent and does not change to align with culture, trends, or public opinion.
- Church leadership is accountable and does not place itself above Scripture or discourage questions.
- Questions are welcomed and encouraged, not shut down through fear, shame, or pressure.
- The focus is on relationship with Jesus, not loyalty to a denomination, leader, or institution.
- Believers are encouraged to read the Bible for themselves, not told to rely solely on church interpretation.
- Fellowship is rooted in love and truth, not control, fear, or isolation from others.

- The fruit of the Spirit is evident over time, including humility, love, patience, and self-control.

A GENTLE REMINDER

If your church does not meet every point on this list, that does not automatically mean you need to leave. Some areas are essential for your spiritual health, while others may be less critical, and careful discernment is needed. This checklist is not meant to create fear or confusion. It is meant to bring clarity.

If you cannot find a Bible-believing church in your immediate area, online options are available. However, Scripture instructs us not to forsake the assembling of believers. You may need to drive a little farther to find a church where you feel spiritually aligned and grounded in the Word.

Pray about it. Ask God for wisdom. Read your Bible. Pay attention to what draws you closer to Jesus and what pulls you away from truth. God is faithful to lead those who seek Him sincerely.

HEALING OUR SOULS . HEALING OUR SOULS . HEALING OUR SOULS . HEALING OUR SOULS .

CHAPTER 6

Regard not them that have familiar spirits, neither seek after wizards, to be defiled by them: I am the LORD your God.

Leviticus 19:31

CHAPTER 6

THE IMPACT OF COUNTERFEIT SPIRITUALITY: RETURNING TO TRUTH

(The Middle Years)

Two years after leaving the church and moving back to Brooklyn, I met Felix, who would become my husband and the father of my children. Meeting him felt like the beginning of a new chapter. Jourdan was born first, and I was ecstatic to finally be a mother. It was something I had always wanted. Two years later, in 2000, Felix and I were married, hopeful and certain we were building something that would last.

In 2002, Olivia was born, and our little family felt complete. I had tried for two years to get pregnant and quietly hoped for a daughter. She was the daughter I wanted. Those early years were full of movement and support. I worked from home, and we were blessed to have family nearby who showed up in practical, loving ways. My sister Marcia was a steady presence, especially with Jourdan. She cared for him as a newborn whenever I needed to run errands, work, or when Felix and I slipped away for a date night. She loved him deeply, and he adored her. He could not quite pronounce Marcia, so he called her Auntie Mo-nie, and the name stuck.

Felix and I truly enjoyed those early years together. We did all the things new couples do. We celebrated weddings, baby showers, and birthdays. Weekends were often spent with Cynthia and Jarry and Michelle and Wayne. We laughed, shared meals, and talked about life while our children played nearby. Those were some of our best years. It felt especially sweet because we were all growing together.

By 2005, when Jourdan was six and Olivia was two, our marriage ended in divorce. Looking back, I can see how ill equipped we were. It is difficult to sustain a marriage when you were never given healthy tools, when you do not understand trauma, healing, or your own emotional wounds. I did the best I could with what I knew at the time, but it was not enough.

After the divorce, I moved from New Jersey to Las Vegas. We lived there for three years, and then relocated to Houston, Texas where we would spend the next sixteen years. Those early years were demanding, and I could not have done it without help. My sister Joan and my father were especially supportive when the children were small. Joan moved with me from New Jersey to Las Vegas to help care for the kids while I worked. It was her second time uprooting her life to support me. My father would come from Jamaica for two to three months at a time to help as well.

We attended several different churches as a family in both Las Vegas and Houston. I did everything I knew how to do to give my children a good life. They were not spoiled, but they wanted for nothing. Jourdan took drum and piano lessons, though this was never really his passion. He tried tee-ball, basketball, and karate, but what he truly loved was dancing. Olivia was involved in ballet, tap, gymnastics, and cheerleading, with a special love for cheer. Many years later, Jourdan would discover wrestling, and he and I fell completely in love with the sport. Olivia would reluctantly follow four years later, eventually falling in love with it too. She would go on to wrestle in college and win many accolades. I had no concerns about my children. They were good kids.

In 2006, while living in Las Vegas, I was introduced to The Secret by Rhonda Byrne. What began as curiosity quickly became obsession. The Secret and the law of attraction took over my life. I straddled two worlds for a while, devouring everything related to manifesting while still occasionally going to church and praying to God. Over time, God was quietly replaced with "the universe." Church attendance became sporadic. Eventually, manifesting became my primary belief system.

Because of the trauma I carried from childhood and the deep sense of having no control, manifesting gave me the illusion of control. I believed that if I could just focus harder, say more affirmations, attend more seminars, write more lists, practice more gratitude, sit under more gurus, listen to more subliminals, then eventually I would have everything my heart desired. I stayed deceived by the Secret, manifesting, and the law of attraction for nearly nineteen years.

None of it delivered what it promised.

I also became fascinated with books like The Da Vinci Code, a fictional conspiracy theory presented as hidden truth, suggesting that Jesus Christ was married to Mary Magdalene and that their descendants were protected by a secret society. Looking back, I can see how hungry I was for mystery, hidden knowledge, and anything that felt empowering or exclusive.

Little by little, I drifted further from the things of God and from what I had learned during my three devoted years in church. The enemy rarely works in obvious ways. It is subtle. Incremental. Like making a salad. A little lettuce here, a few tomatoes, cucumbers, avocado, then protein. Before you realize it, you have a full meal. That is how deception works.

I am deeply grateful that God never gave up on me, even when I walked far away from Him. If this sounds familiar to you, please hear this with love and clarity.

Scripture tells us that Satan is the god of this world. So if you're manifesting, treating God like a genie in a bottle, asking for whatever you want without thinking about why He created you or what His will is, and you actually get it, remember this: not everything we receive is truly from God.

We cannot reduce God to a formula. We cannot box Him in or manipulate Him. That posture is not faith. It is entitlement. When the words manifest, manifested, or manifestation appear in the Bible, they mean something very different than what is taught in New Age spirituality. Biblically, to manifest is to make something known, visible, or clear, especially the presence or work of God. It is not a technique to create outcomes.

Manifesting as it is taught today is not a Christian principle. It is New Age. The focus is self-empowerment through thoughts, visualization, scripting, and trying to control what is often called "the universe." God created the universe. God and the universe are not the same. When we put creation above the Creator, we are elevating the wrong thing.

There are Christians sitting in churches every Sunday who are deeply involved in manifesting. This is not harmless. It is not neutral. It is a warning sign that there may be a turning away from reliance on God and seeking control through our own efforts instead of trusting His will.

Gratitude becomes a transaction rather than worship. Thanksgiving is offered not from the heart but as a tool to get more. That is manipulation, not relationship. When I followed the Law of Attraction and New Age teachings, I felt completely disconnected from God, even while believing I was becoming more spiritual.

I wasn't ascending. I was drifting. The Law of Attraction teaches that our thoughts alone can create reality. Positive thoughts are meant to bring blessings, and negative thoughts are said to bring disaster. This can make a person hyper-focused on every passing thought, anxious about attracting something unwanted, and trapped in a cycle of fear and control. In contrast, scripture teaches that life and death are in the power of the tongue, not in obsessive self-focused thinking. God calls us to trust Him, not to manipulate outcomes with our minds.

Following is a list of common New Age terms, beliefs, and practices, alongside biblical truth. This comparison is intended to clarify the difference between New Age teachings and God's Word and to help you recognize what aligns with His will.

NEW AGE PRACTICES COMPARED WITH BIBLICAL TRUTH (ALPHABETICAL)

New Age Term	New Age Definition	Biblical Truth with Scripture
Angel Cards	Cards believed to deliver messages from angels for guidance or reassurance.	Angels are ministering spirits sent by God. We are never instructed to seek messages from angels. Worship or reliance on angels is warned against in Scripture. (Hebrews 1:14; Colossians 2:18)
Ascension	The belief that humanity evolves into higher spiritual dimensions or consciousness.	Scripture teaches sanctification through surrender and obedience, not spiritual selfelevation. (Romans 12:1–2; Philippians 2:8–9)
Astral Traveling	Conscious separation of spirit from the body to access other realms.	Seeking supernatural realms outside God's authority is forbidden. God alone controls spiritual access. (Isaiah 8:19; Colossians 2:18)
Christ Consciousness	The belief that Jesus reached divine awareness that humans can also attain.	Jesus is not an enlightened teacher. He is the Son of God, fully divine and fully human. We follow Christ; we do not become Christ. (John 1:1–14; Colossians 1:15–19)
Crystals	Objects believed to store, transmit, or amplify spiritual energy.	Assigning power to objects is idolatry. Our trust and source must be God alone. (Isaiah 42:8; Psalm 20:7)

New Age Term	New Age Definition	Biblical Truth with Scripture
Empath	A spiritual identity claiming heightened ability to absorb others' emotions or energy.	Compassion is biblical, but absorbing emotional or spiritual energy is not. Many who identify as empaths are actually operating from trauma and hypervigilance. God invites us to cast burdens on Him. (Matthew 11:28; 1 Peter 5:7)
Energy Healing	Healing through manipulation or channeling of universal energy.	Healing comes from God alone. Any power not sourced from Him is counterfeit. (Psalm 103:2–3; Isaiah 53:5)
Evil Eye	The belief that envy or attention can cause spiritual harm.	God is our protector. Fearbased superstition is not from Him. (Psalm 121; 2 Timothy 1:7)
Florida Water	A scented liquid used for spiritual cleansing or protection rituals.	Ritual cleansing apart from Christ **is no longer required**. True cleansing comes through repentance and salvation. (1 John 1:7; Hebrews 9:14)
Goddess Worship	Reverence of divine feminine deities or feminine spiritual energy.	Women are created in God's image, but worship belongs to God alone. (Genesis 1:27; Exodus 20:3–5)
High Frequency / Vibration	Measuring spirituality by vibrational level or energetic frequency.	Spiritual maturity is measured by fruit, obedience, and holiness, not vibration. (Galatians 5:22–23; John 14:15)

New Age Term	New Age Definition	Biblical Truth with Scripture
Horoscopes / Astrology	Seeking guidance or identity through stars and planetary alignment.	God forbids looking to the stars for guidance. He alone orders our steps. (Isaiah 47:13–14; Jeremiah 10:2)
Kundalini Awakening	A coiled spiritual energy believed to rise through the body to produce enlightenment.	The Holy Spirit brings peace, order, and clarity, not forced bodily awakening. (1 Corinthians 14:33; John 14:26)
Mercury Retrograde	The belief that planetary movement causes disruption or misfortune.	No planet governs a believer's life. God is sovereign over time and events. (Proverbs 16:9; Romans 8:28)
Numerology / Angel Numbers	Use of numbers for selfdiscovery, divination, and predicting future events.	Numbers symbolize divine concepts (7 = perfection, 40 = testing, 12 = authority/ God's people). They are **not** secret codes to predict or control life. (Leviticus 4:6–7; Exodus 24:18; Matthew 4:2; Revelation 21:12)
Oracle Cards	Cards used to receive spiritual insight or future guidance.	Divination is forbidden. God invites us to seek Him directly. (Deuteronomy 18:10; Proverbs 3:5–6)
Past Lives	The belief that souls live multiple lifetimes for growth or karma.	Scripture teaches one life, then judgment. (Hebrews 9:27; Ezekiel 18:20)

New Age Term	New Age Definition	Biblical Truth with Scripture
Pendulum	A tool used to receive yes or no answers from spiritual forces.	This is divination. God provides wisdom through prayer and His Word. (James 1:5; Deuteronomy 18:10)
Psychic	A person believed to access hidden knowledge or predict the future apart from God.	Scripture forbids psychic practices. Prophets wait on God and speak only what He reveals. (Deuteronomy 18:10–12; 2 Peter 1:21; 1 Corinthians 14:3)
Reiki	A healing practice involving channeling universal life energy.	God heals through His power alone. Reiki channels power apart from God. (Mark 16:17–18; Acts 3:6; James 5:14–16)
Saging	Burning herbs to cleanse people or spaces of negative energy.	Scripture teaches cleansing through repentance and submission to God, not rituals. (James 4:7; Psalm 91)
Soulmate / Twin Flame	The belief that another person completes you spiritually.	Wholeness comes from God, not another person. Twin flame ideology often excuses toxic relationships. (Colossians 2:10; Jeremiah 17:5)
Spells	Rituals intended to manipulate outcomes or reality.	Attempting to control reality through ritual is witchcraft. Prayer submits to God's will. (Galatians 5:19–21; Matthew 6:10)

New Age Term	New Age Definition	Biblical Truth with Scripture
Spirit Guides	Nonphysical beings believed to offer guidance or protection.	Seeking guidance from spirits is condemned. Guidance comes from the Holy Spirit and Scripture. (Deuteronomy 18:10–12; John 16:13)
Star Seed	Belief that some humans originate from other star systems.	Humans are created by God, from the earth, in His image. (Genesis 1:27; Genesis 2:7)
Tarot Cards	Cards used to predict the future or reveal hidden truth.	Tarot is divination and opens the door to deception. God alone reveals truth. (Deuteronomy 18:10–12; Psalm 119:105)

A NOTE FROM MY JOURNEY

I want to be clear and honest here. I was deceived by many of these practices for years. As you can see, nearly all of them are counterfeits of God's gifts, God's Word, and God's design for relationship with Him. The only practice I never engaged in was Kundalini awakening. Even then, something about it felt frightening and unsafe, and I stayed away from it.

You may genuinely have been given gifts from God, but that does not mean those gifts are being used to honor Him or in the way He intended. Satan sees God-given gifts and attempts to pervert them for his own purposes. Scripture reminds us that every good and perfect gift comes from God and adds no sorrow. (James 1:17; Proverbs 10:22)

A few years before I fully gave my life to the Lord, I briefly explored Kemetic and Ancient Egyptian spirituality. The woman I spoke with was the first person who told me I had the gift of healing. She strongly encouraged me to join her religion. Something about it did not sit right with my spirit, and I walked away.

Later, taking matters into my own hands, I pursued Reiki and became attuned. At the time, I believed I was developing a God-given gift. After rededicating my life to Christ, I renounced Reiki and all agreements connected to it.

I also want to address twin flame teachings directly. Twin flame language often justifies remaining in toxic relationships. Concepts like runner and chaser create a spiritual explanation for dysfunction, trauma bonding, and emotional unavailability. God does not call us to stay bound to relationships that harm us in the name of spiritual destiny.

I remember working on a project while employed at Citibank in my early twenties, when a colleague joked that it must be Mercury retrograde because we kept having to revise slides. He explained the concept, and I ran with it for years, blaming disruptions, confusion, and setbacks on planetary movement. Thank God I am free from that thinking.

The term empath is especially popular in New Age spaces. It convinced me that I had a special spiritual ability, when in truth I was traumatized and hypervigilant. I had learned to read emotional shifts in others as a survival skill. What I once called a gift was actually a protective mechanism.

If you recognize yourself here, you are not alone. This is part of my healing journey, one that required honesty, repentance, and compassion toward myself.

PRAYER TO RENOUNCE NEW AGE INVOLVEMENT

Father God,

I come before You with humility and gratitude. I acknowledge that many of these practices were entered into with sincere intentions. I was seeking healing, clarity, peace, and control in places where only You can truly provide them. Your Word reminds me to trust in You with all my heart and not lean on my own understanding, knowing that You alone make my paths straight (Proverbs 3:5–6).

I repent for seeking wisdom, power, identity, or healing apart from You, whether knowingly or unknowingly. I renounce every belief, practice, agreement, and influence listed here that does not come from You. I break alignment with anything counterfeit, deceptive, or contrary to Your Word, choosing to be rooted and established in Christ rather than taken captive by hollow or deceptive philosophies (Colossians 2:8).

In the Name of Jesus, I renounce all involvement with New Age and occult practices, including divination, false spiritual identities, energy-based healing, astrology, manifesting, and any form of spiritual authority apart from You. I ask You to cleanse me, restore me, and realign every part of my life with Your truth.

I declare that Jesus Christ is my Lord, my Savior, my healer, and my source. I receive the Holy Spirit as my guide and submit my gifts fully to You, to be used only in ways that honor You and bring life.

Thank You for Your mercy, Your patience, and Your faithfulness. Thank You that You redeem what was misused and restore what was surrendered. I choose truth, freedom, and obedience to You alone.

In Jesus' Name. Amen.

HEALING OUR SOULS . HEALING OUR SOULS . HEALING OUR SOULS . HEALING OUR SOULS .

CHAPTER 7

Keep thy heart with all diligence; for out of it are the issues of life.

Proverbs 4:23

CHAPTER 7

GUARD YOUR HEART

After my first divorce in 2005, we moved to Las Vegas for three years. In August 2008, after the Las Vegas real estate market crashed, we relocated again, this time to Houston. The brand-new home I had purchased for $450,000 was now worth $200,000. Almost overnight, I found myself in serious financial distress.

As a writing consultant, work dried up, and I could no longer afford the mortgage on a home that had lost more than half its value. A friend in Houston told me the city had no state income tax and a lower cost of living, so I made the difficult decision to walk away from our beautiful new home with its custom-built pool. I traded in my expensive minivan for a fifteen-year-old four-door sedan that my brother Donovan graciously gave me.

Jourdan, Olivia, my father, and I packed what we could fit and drove the twenty-four hours from Las Vegas to Houston in that car, pulling a small U-Haul with the rest of our belongings. I was financially bankrupt, but not emotionally broken. The kids were six and ten, and they saw the whole thing as an adventure. They never complained.

At the time, I had about one hundred dollars in my bank account, less than fifty dollars from coins I cashed in, and a stack of McDonald's coupons. That is how we survived. My father, a Jamaican citizen, did not have a United States driver's license, so I did all the driving. We stopped once or twice at rest stops to get a few hours of sleep before getting back on the road.

We had two mattresses strapped to the top of the car and the U-Haul hitched behind us. I was driving as if the car was not pulling anything at all. Within forty-five minutes, the car started smoking and stalling. I immediately prayed it was not the transmission. We pulled over, my father added water to the radiator, and we prayed that God would get us to our destination safely. Then we got back on the road. God heard our prayers, and we made it to Houston without further issues.

We moved into a modest two-bedroom apartment in the neighborhood where I wanted my children to attend school. Jourdan and Olivia shared a room and could not have been happier. My brother Donovan and his wife Laura loaned me money so I could pay rent for a few months while I looked for work.

For the first time in my life, I applied for and received food stamps. It was truly a blessing. I also received help from Northwest Assistance Ministries in Houston, which provided food and support, especially around Thanksgiving and Christmas. They even allowed each child to pick out two gifts from donated items. I will always be grateful for that kindness, and one day I hope to donate a million dollars to that life-saving organization.

My sisters Marcia and Angela sent money for Christmas gifts, which lifted a tremendous burden. We were able to have a joyful Christmas, and my children never once complained about what we had lost. We were grateful for everything God provided through family, community organizations, and government assistance.

My kids actually loved apartment living because there were so many other children to play with. One of the things I have always admired most about them is their gratitude, regardless of circumstances.

Around that time, a dear friend named Katherine received a new opportunity and referred me for the consulting job she was leaving. The position paid well and was with a company based in Canada, which allowed me to work remotely. Within a few months, I was back on my feet financially and able to repay the money I had borrowed.

THE SIFTING CONTINUES

Everything in my life seemed to be going along just fine, at least on the surface. I had not dealt with my childhood wounds or past pain, and like most people, I did not think it was a problem. I was functioning, working, providing, and moving forward. I did not have any major complaints. What I did not realize was that unresolved pain does not disappear. It waits.

In 2010, I married a Believer who I met online who was living in Nigeria. I traveled there for his visa interview, and quite literally, that is when all hell broke loose.

What had been lying dormant for years was suddenly brought to the surface by an incident that occurred on September 11, 2011, when I nearly died from a pulmonary embolism while returning from Nigeria and changing planes at Washington Dulles Airport. It was the perfect storm.

Four days before my trip, I had fallen and developed a pinhead-sized blood clot on my left toe along with a scraped knee. I was also taking a friend's birth control pills so I would not get my period during the visit, and I was rubbing an over-the-counter progesterone cream on my body to keep it firm. At the time, I thought nothing of any of it.

When I arrived in Nigeria, I felt a little off, but after a day or two I started feeling like myself again. Five days later, I boarded a twelve-hour flight home with very little rest. I was so exhausted that I did not get up even once. Looking back, I believe that was God protecting me.

Early in the flight, I felt a sharp cramp in my left leg. I ignored it and went back to sleep. When the plane landed and I stood up, I felt nauseous. My left leg was swollen from my ankle to my calf, and I knew something was wrong.

As I made my way off the plane, I struggled to carry my bag and felt extremely winded. I remember thinking, when did I get so out of shape that walking and carrying a bag leaves me this breathless?

I was sweating profusely, my heart was racing, and I felt deeply unsettled. I thought if I could just make it to the bathroom and put a cold towel on my head, I would snap out of it. I even wondered if I was overreacting.

But once I was in the stall, I knew something was very wrong. I called out to the woman next to me and asked her to get help. Within minutes, the medics arrived. As I stood up and opened the stall door, I blacked out.

In that moment, I silently cried out to Jesus and told Him I did not want to die.

The medic asked me questions and I mentioned malaria, but he said my symptoms did not align. I asked if I was having a heart attack, and he said he did not think so. They cared for me in the ambulance and did everything they could to keep me calm.

At the hospital, the doctor suspected a pulmonary embolism and ordered tests to confirm it. The results showed blood clots traveling to both sides of my lungs. He told me he sees cases like this often due to long flights and said it was a miracle that I survived. I give God all the glory for saving my life. He orchestrated every detail so that I could leave that airport alive.

At that time, I had only been working for an oil and gas company for four months. When they learned what had happened, the Vice President of Human Resources sent someone to retrieve my luggage from the airport. When I returned to work a few days later, she made me a full-time employee. It remains one of the kindest acts anyone has ever extended to me. Senior leaders and coworkers were genuinely happy to see me back.

They say demons feed off fear, and my fear after that incident was overwhelming. I did not want to die on the bathroom floor of an airport, far away from my children who were nine and thirteen at the time. The thought of leaving them without me gripped my heart.

God, in His sovereignty, even provided continuity in my care. The doctor who treated me had a brother who was a physician in Houston. He referred me to him, and that brother became my doctor for the next thirteen years.

I was placed on blood thinners for three months, and it took a long time for my body to feel normal again. While my body healed, my mind did not. I developed anxiety and became hyper-aware of every unfamiliar sensation in my body. That near-death experience awakened fear and PTSD that had been lying dormant since childhood.

In early 2012, my Nigerian husband came to the United States. Being far from his family, unable to work, and without his own income weighed heavily on him. We attended church together and sought marital counseling, but nothing brought lasting change.

During that time, my husband sought counsel from his Christian family in Nigeria. From their perspective, they felt we were facing spiritual challenges and suggested that family dynamics, including jealousy and envy, could create openings for difficulty. I dismissed what he shared and assumed it was an excuse for him not taking responsibility for his behavior. I also could not imagine anyone being jealous of me. I did not feel successful, secure, or settled. I was still recovering physically and emotionally from a near-death experience.

The truth is, aside from my sister Joan, I did not tell the rest of my family I was getting married until after it happened. I was protecting my peace, having experienced rejection years earlier while pregnant, and I could not bear to walk through that kind of hurt again. At the same time, I recognize that my loved ones may have been concerned about my choices, especially given patterns I had shown in the past.

Looking back, my marriage was complicated and fragile for many reasons, some external and some my own. Within eleven months of my husband arriving in the United States, we separated, and we would later divorce three years after that. At the time, I could not clearly see why everything was unraveling so quickly. With reflection, I see that both of us were navigating challenges we were not fully equipped to manage, and that God used the season to teach me deeper lessons about myself, boundaries, and trust.

JEALOUSY AND ENVY

I'd like to take a moment to talk about jealousy and envy, emotions we have all felt at some point. When left unexamined, they are powerful forces, and Scripture is clear about the harm they can cause. Proverbs 14:30 tells us that envy rots the bones. James 3:16 says that where envy and selfish ambition exist, there is disorder and every evil practice. These are not harmless emotions. They are destructive, eroding relationships and creating insecurity, anxiety, and resentment for the person experiencing them. They can also affect the recipient, sometimes leading to emotional exhaustion, manipulation, or conflict.

Jealousy and envy can show up in many ways. We might feel it when someone receives a promotion, buys a new home or car, celebrates a milestone, starts a family, or achieves something we desire for ourselves. It can appear as comparison, judgment, entitlement, or even as the need to interfere in someone else's choices. It can also show up quietly as bitterness, withdrawal, or fear of being fully seen. Recognizing these emotions in ourselves is the first step toward freedom.

It is essential to examine ourselves and seek God's guidance so that our hearts and decisions are healthy and rooted in truth. If we find ourselves the target of jealousy or envy, it is important to set boundaries and protect our well-being, while also remembering that everyone has the right to live their life without interference or scrutiny, as long as they are not causing harm.

We often envy what we see on the surface without understanding the sacrifices, losses, or private battles that brought someone to where they are. What looks effortless on the outside may have required great endurance on the inside. God has not called us to compete with one another. He has called us to trust Him. Psalm 139 reminds us that we are fearfully and wonderfully made, each with a purpose designed specifically for us. Comparison, jealousy, and envy distract us from our own assignment. Trust God and trust yourself enough to believe that what He has for you is custom designed. It will not look like anyone else's, and it does not need to.

Before continuing, I invite you to pause and reflect.

REFLECTION

Jealousy and envy are not always loud. Sometimes they show up as disappointment, entitlement, comparison, or the need to stay closely involved in someone else's choices. Other times, they show up as secrecy, withdrawal, or the fear of being fully seen. God does not expose these things to punish us, but to heal us. When we allow Him to search our hearts, He does so with compassion.

JOURNAL PROMPTS

Take your time with these questions. There are no right or wrong answers.

1. **Have I ever felt hurt, threatened, or left behind** by someone else's progress, joy, or decisions? What emotions came up for me in those moments?

2. **Have I ever minimized someone else's happiness** or questioned their choices because it made me uncomfortable or afraid?

3. **In what ways might I have benefited from stronger boundaries,** either setting them or respecting them?

4. **Have there been times when I felt judged, controlled, or unsupported** by others when making decisions for my own life? How did that affect me?

5. **Ask God gently,** Lord, is there any jealousy, envy, or comparison in my heart that You want to heal? Sit with whatever comes up without judgment.

As Proverbs 4:23 reminds us, we are to guard our hearts, for everything we do flows from them. Guarding our hearts does not mean closing them. It means allowing God access to the places we would rather avoid.

HEALING OUR SOULS · HEALING OUR SOULS · HEALING OUR SOULS · HEALING OUR SOULS ·

CHAPTER 8

But I am poor and sorrowful: let thy salvation,
O God, set me up on high.

Psalm 69:29

CHAPTER 8

THE BREAKING POINT

I got a great job in 2011. My Nigerian husband came to the United States in February 2012. We moved into a brand-new construction home in October of that year. By January 2013, we were separated. The divorce was finalized in 2015.

The house was in a nice neighborhood, in a great school district. On paper, everything looked right. I truly believed I was making wise and responsible decisions. I was deeply devoted to my children. There were no men coming in and out of our home. I did not smoke, use drugs, and only drank socially. I attended church most Sundays. I worked from home until my children were nine and thirteen, and during their younger years I made sure trusted family members were present while I worked. We were fortunate enough to be able to travel out of the country every year.

Jourdan discovered wrestling as a freshman in high school, and our lives quickly revolved around practices and tournaments. We spent countless hours together as a family. Olivia and Jourdan were not allowed to date until sixteen because I remembered how distracting boys had been when I discovered them too early in life.

Looking back, I see how intentional I was. I was trying to build a life that felt safe, stable, and protected, especially after so much instability in my own childhood. Scripture says, "Unless the Lord builds the house, those who build it labor in vain" (Psalm 127:1). At the time, I did not recognize how much of that building I was doing on my own.

We spent nearly every weekend together as a family. Then one Saturday something changed in me. I expected our usual mall run followed by dinner. Instead, Jourdan told me he had a date. Olivia had been invited to her best friend's house, the triplets. I remember standing there feeling suddenly abandoned and deeply alone. In that moment, I realized my children were no longer little. They were growing up. They wanted independence. They had discovered lives that did not revolve around me.

Jourdan was driving at sixteen and had his own car. This season was particularly difficult for me because I could no longer guarantee their safety. They were not with me all the time, and I did not always know where they were or what they were doing. I worried constantly. What I did not understand then was that I had made my children an idol. I had placed myself in the role of God in their lives, believing that if I loved them enough and protected them enough, I could shield them from pain. I never truly turned my children over to God. I did not trust Him because I had not been protected. The only protector I knew was myself. Yet Scripture reminds us, "Cast all your anxiety on Him because He cares for you" (1 Peter 5:7).

JOURNAL PROMPTS

Have you ever confused love with control?

What is God inviting you to release back into His hands?

SCRIPTURE

Cast all your care on Him for He cares for you - 1 Peter 5:7

TORMENTED BY PANIC ATTACKS

During this time, I began experiencing panic attacks connected to the pulmonary embolism and near-death experience. My body no longer felt safe to me. Everything startled me. Everything worried me. I struggled with periods of insomnia, and at one point developed vertigo that lasted for a week or two. The doctor could not explain the cause and told me it would likely resolve on its own, which it eventually did.

My diet also shifted, and I suddenly lost the desire to eat meat. As I shared earlier, I had been increasingly exposed to New Age beliefs, and I began interpreting these symptoms through that lens. When I searched online, I found explanations describing what was referred to as a spiritual awakening. These teachings framed anxiety, dizziness, sleep disruption, and appetite changes as signs of heightened awareness or spiritual expansion. Discomfort was presented not as something to be treated, but as evidence of growth.

What I did not understand at the time was that these same symptoms are also common during perimenopause. Medical science identifies them as the result of fluctuating hormones, including estrogen, progesterone, and testosterone, which affect nearly every system in a woman's body. These changes can last eight to ten years. In my confusion, I spiritualized what was happening in my body and my nervous system instead of seeking practical, informed care. Scripture says, "My people perish for lack of knowledge" (Hosea 4:6).

I did attempt to get medical help. My general practitioner suggested antidepressants for the anxiety and wrote a prescription. I took it for a few days but stopped. I was terrified of medication because of experiences I had in my early twenties, and I feared dependence and the idea that stopping would require a long tapering process. I also explored bioidentical hormones but was advised against them due to the increased risk of blood clots, given my history of pulmonary embolism. I felt stuck, frightened, and unsure where to turn.

DIVORCED AND DECEIVED

After my second divorce, I returned to online dating after a few months, still searching for relief from loneliness and pain. Around that time, a man connected to my job reached out to me and shared that he had seen my dating profile. There had always been a mutual attraction between us when we were both single. Now I was divorced, and he had been married less than a year.

That conversation marked the beginning of a six-year cycle of flirtation and emotional entanglement. We played a quiet game of cat and mouse, with the roles shifting depending on our circumstances and emotional needs. We never crossed the line physically because one of us would eventually pull back, recognizing that an affair would be wrong. But emotionally, boundaries were crossed again and again.

I became deeply attached to his attention and words. I fantasized about a future that was never actually available. While he may have cared for me as a friend, this was never going to become a committed partnership. He eventually got divorced, but not because of me. I was starving for love and attached myself to any man who showed consistency, kindness, or interest. Scripture warns us, “Above all else, guard your heart, for everything you do flows from it” (Proverbs 4:23). At the time, I was guarding my loneliness more than my heart.

There was a season when I would never have entertained flirtation with a married man. But distance from God rarely happens all at once. It happens gradually. Without accountability, conviction softens. Sin becomes normalized. It is often reinforced by culture, celebrated in entertainment, and left unchallenged without wise counsel. Over time, the conscience dulls. No matter how intelligent, accomplished, or outwardly confident a person may appear, unhealed wounds will always influence their choices.

SOBERING REALIZATION

Around this time, I had a sobering realization. I was the one constant in all of my failed relationships. Determined to fix myself, I immersed myself in learning everything I could about men and dating. I joined a year-long relationship mastermind at a discounted cost of ten thousand dollars. While emotional wounds were briefly mentioned, I bypassed that work, focused instead on learning how to attract, communicate with, and keep men. The information never integrated. Nothing changed except my bank account.

In my desperation, I moved from one relationship coach to another. I consumed free and paid content relentlessly. I visited astrologers, paid for compatibility charts, participated in past-life regressions, listened to subliminals, and spent thousands of dollars on psychic love readings. I was willing to do anything to secure love. Slowly, God was replaced with methods, formulas, and spiritual substitutes. I drifted further from the God of Abraham, Isaac, and Jacob, even as Scripture reminds us, “Trust in the Lord with all your heart and lean not on your own understanding” (Proverbs 3:5).

The truth I could not yet see was that I was addicted to the pursuit of love. I believed that the right man would arrive and finally make me feel safe, chosen, and whole. I placed expectations on men that no human being could fulfill. It took many years to understand that Jesus is the only perfect man and the only true Savior. I had been trying to manage my future and heal my past through relationships after a lifetime marked by instability and loss.

It was not until late 2023 and early 2024 that I fully grasped how deeply traumatized I was. No amount of learning how to text correctly, perform confidence, or present myself as high value was ever going to heal what was broken inside me. Healing required honesty, surrender, and a return to God, not as a concept, but as my source.

JOURNAL PROMPTS

Who or what have you expected to save you besides Jesus?

SCRIPTURE

Come to Me, all who are weary and burdened, and I will give you rest. - Matthew 11:28

HEALING OUR SOULS . HEALING OUR SOULS . HEALING OUR SOULS . HEALING OUR SOULS .

CHAPTER 9

Children are a heritage from the LORD, offspring a reward from him.

Psalm 127:3

CHAPTER 9

CHILDREN ARE A BLESSING FROM GOD

JOURDAN'S STORY

I was riding the New York City subway one day before I had children when I noticed a mother and her son, maybe ten years old. I could see the love and connection between them. Something in me whispered a prayer. I remember thinking, *I want that kind of relationship with my son someday.* God answered that prayer in Jourdan.

From the very beginning, there was a deep bond between us. Less than twenty-four hours after he was born, Jourdan lay in the bassinet beside my hospital bed. I was exhausted, my hand resting over the edge of the bassinet. He reached up, wrapped his tiny fingers around mine, and locked eyes with me. In that moment, I felt a deep connection.

As a baby and toddler, Jourdan never wanted to be far from me. If I left the room, he cried. Years later, while talking with my friend Gail from Las Vegas about men and their relationships with their mothers, she said, "Your son loves you deeply. I can see it in the way he looks at you and how he treats you." Jourdan's friends would say the same. Even today, they tell me, "Jourdan loved his mama and his sister."

Jourdan was one of those kids who seemed to be friends with everyone. The popular kids. The quiet kids. The ones who did not quite fit anywhere else. He loved to talk and occasionally got notes sent home for talking too much in class. He liked to have a good time. He was what I would call a party-like-a-rock-star kind of personality.

Much later, Jourdan shared with me that as a young boy he was influenced by rap and trap music that glamorized recreational drug use and a fast lifestyle. Although I introduced him to Christian rap artists, he listened to other music outside the home. Like many kids raised in good homes, he was drawn to the image of "success" that surrounded him. Hustle culture. Becoming a millionaire by thirty. Popping bottles. Parties. Social media amplified it all.

While he was far from perfect, Jourdan had a tender heart. He loved being around family and often asked when we would take another family vacation. The last one had been in 2016 when he graduated from high school. We stopped traveling internationally because that money was needed for his college education.

In the year before he passed, Jourdan reconnected with his father and healed a separation that had lasted far too long. He spent Thanksgiving with me, his aunt Angela, and his cousin Kristin and her family just one week before he passed, on December 1, 2023. In many ways, he was deeply blessed.

Jourdan also coached youth wrestling and impacted countless children and families. Through those relationships, he grew in his understanding of God and Jesus. As I was exploring different churches, one of the last things he said to me was, "Mom, do not mess with anything that takes away from Jesus and what He did on the cross."

In his final group text to Olivia and me, he encouraged us to do something kind for others. Jourdan was not an angel. He had his struggles and his share of trouble. But he was kind. He had a sensitive spirit.

I had written earlier about an inner knowing, a way God sometimes speaks to me quietly but clearly. I felt that knowing again when Jourdan was home for Thanksgiving. Watching him play with his dog, Harmony, something settled in my spirit. I knew he was too tender to remain here much longer. My sister later said I have a knowing. I believe she is right.

When I dropped him off at the airport, I heard a quiet instruction inside. Get out of the car and really hug him. This may be the last time. I obeyed. God was preparing me, even then, for what was coming.

When I received the call five days later, I heard the Spirit of God say, "This is the day you have worried about." In that instant, every fear I had ever carried about raising a young Black man in this world vanished. I was filled with peace. I was not angry with God. I did not ask why. Somehow, I knew it was simply time.

A few months earlier, during a walk, I had tried to negotiate with God. I said, "If you heal my son, I will do what You called me to do and help heal Your people." God has a way of answering us when we tell Him what we will do.

Jourdan and I had talked about healing the issues in our bloodline together. I did not know then how that conversation would be fulfilled. This book itself is a testimony to the healing work God has done in me. Scripture reminds us, "Many are the plans in a person's heart, but it is the Lord's purpose that prevails" (Proverbs 19:21).

OLIVIA'S STORY

Years before Olivia was born, I was at a park with Jourdan and Felix, my husband at the time. I noticed a beautiful little girl with wavy hair pulled into a slick ponytail. My heart leapt. I remember thinking, *I want my daughter to look like that.*

Olivia arrived as a beautiful, big baby girl, nearly ten pounds. I named her after my mother, Olive. To this day, she wears her hair slicked back in a wavy ponytail, just like the little girl I once admired.

Wherever I went with my children, people commented on how beautiful they were and how well behaved. Jourdan immediately fell in love with his baby sister, four years his junior. Jourdan and I often joked that Olivia was the best of the three of us. She seemed fearless and excelled at everything she tried. She danced at five, joined cheerleading younger than most of the girls on the team, and performed a solo ballet at six. She was disciplined, mild mannered, and deeply talented.

Olivia attempted things Jourdan and I never had the courage to try: acting, singing, and putting herself out there. We marveled at her confidence and focus. When she fell in love with cheerleading and gymnastics, we encouraged her to wrestle as well. It was not her passion, but she did it to please us. She excelled anyway.

She placed third in the state, helped her high school team become the first state champions, placed fourth at Fargo, and earned a national ranking. She received an athletic scholarship to wrestle in college, became an All American, helped her college team win three national duals championships, and continues working toward an individual national championship.

At sixteen, Olivia began dating, and this marked a shift. I was an overprotective mother. I trusted very few people with my children. My own experiences with betrayal shaped that fear.

At first, the relationship seemed good. Over time, I noticed changes. Olivia began losing matches she once dominated, while her boyfriend's success and visibility increased. I blurted out one day that he was stealing her shine. At the time, it sounded strange even to me. Later, I came to understand it more clearly as a dynamic where emotional manipulation and comparison slowly erode another person's confidence. Scripture tells us that the thief comes to steal, kill, and destroy (John 10:10), and sometimes that theft begins with identity and self-worth.

Behind the scenes, he cheated on her and undermined her confidence, telling her that others did not like her or think she was a good wrestler. Her self-esteem suffered. She did not tell me what was happening. She graduated high school in 2020 during COVID. There was no prom. She did not make it to the state tournament. Their grandfather passed away that April.

Olivia was grieving deeply, though I did not fully understand the depth of it at the time.

I noticed mood swings and anger and assumed it was hormonal. I took her to the pediatrician. I did not yet realize how much the relationship was contributing.

In 2020, there was an unprecedented surge in collective anger, profound sadness, and a pervasive sense of fear. I purchased a gun and made the grave mistake of not securing it properly. Olivia, devastated by betrayal, told her boyfriend she was considering harming herself. Thankfully, he insisted she tell me. I immediately got her into therapy.

She minimized what was happening, attributing her feelings to grief. Two or three months later, she left for college.

In February 2021, I visited her. Her coach believed she was depressed. The next day, I received a call that shattered me. Olivia had been hospitalized after attempting to harm herself with medication. She was fourteen hours away in another state. I boarded the next plane.

Because she was over eighteen, I was given limited information. She spent nights on a ward with adult men and women, surrounded by screaming and chaos. She was nineteen. Eventually, she was moved to a ward with younger women, and I finally exhaled.

After her release, she stayed with me in a hotel. We arranged outpatient therapy and medical care. Olivia was later diagnosed with Premenstrual Dysphoric Disorder, a severe hormonal condition that can cause intense depression, anxiety, irritability, and suicidal thoughts. I later learned that other members of our family had struggled with depression and social anxiety as well. Had I understood our family history earlier, it may have helped with awareness and prevention.

Recovery was long and uneven. Olivia chose to remain in college, believing structure would help. I monitored her closely. Over time, she shared more about the relationship. It was a soul tie that needed to be broken. Scripture reminds us that unhealthy bonds can weigh down the soul, and that God desires freedom for His children (Isaiah 61:1).

I was terrified for both of my children. I did not yet understand spiritual warfare or generational patterns. Fear consumed me.

Weeks before Jourdan passed, Olivia told me she had dreamed of his death multiple times. I brushed it off. Looking back, I wonder what might have changed had I understood more.

After Jourdan's passing, I encouraged Olivia to take time off and come home. She resisted, unwilling to disappoint her team. With the help of her coach, she agreed. Those six months were healing for both of us.

Olivia's story is a reminder to pay attention to those who appear the strongest. The disciplined ones. The achievers. The ones who carry themselves with confidence and rarely ask for help. They are often the most overlooked. You never truly know what someone is carrying beneath the surface, even when they seem to be thriving.

PRAYER OVER CHILDREN

If you have children, are planning to have children, or are a caretaker of children, I encourage you to pray over them often. This is not only for young children, but also for those who are grown, married, or living independently. It is never too early and never too late to pray for our children. Spiritual covering is lifelong.

Heavenly Father,

I lift my children to You. Your Word says that children are a heritage from the Lord, and I entrust them back into Your care (Psalm 127:3). Guard their hearts and minds in Christ Jesus, and protect them from every scheme of the enemy (Philippians 4:7, Ephesians 6:11).

Order their steps according to Your Word, and let Your Spirit guide them in all truth (Psalm 119:133, John 16:13). Surround them with Your angels and keep them in all their ways (Psalm 91:11). May they walk in truth, wisdom, and integrity all the days of their lives.

Lord, draw them close to You. Let them know You intimately, love You deeply, and follow You faithfully. When they wander, call them back. When they are weary, strengthen them. When I cannot be near, cover them with Your presence and power. Fulfill Your will and purpose in their lives, for You have plans to prosper them and not to harm them, to give them a future and a hope (Jeremiah 29:11).

In Jesus' Name. Amen.

HEALING OUR SOULS · HEALING OUR SOULS · HEALING OUR SOULS · HEALING OUR SOULS ·

CHAPTER 10

And be not conformed to this world: but be ye transformed by the renewing of your mind, that ye may prove what is that good, and acceptable, and perfect, will of God.

Romans 12:2

CHAPTER 10

A NEW BEGINNING

Before Jourdan passed, I had planned to move to Las Vegas after retirement to live with my sister Joan. She was with me on a women's retreat when I received the call about Jourdan. I now see that as God's mercy. I did not have to walk through that moment alone.

As Olivia prepared to return to college in Georgia, I began to sense a leading to move there to support her. I had never considered Georgia before, but the truth is that we needed each other to heal after losing our beloved Jourdan. Though I initially resisted the idea, God allowed stressful circumstances at the job I had been at for thirteen years to bring that season to an end and make the move possible.

Though I made the decision to retire, I felt pushed out. At the time, it felt deeply unfair. I had invested so much of myself, and for it to end the way it did was painful and disorienting. I felt like a failure. I felt unseen and uncared for, especially after everything I had already endured. I believed more empathy should have been given, and the absence of it created its own wound. I carried those feelings for many months.

In hindsight, I can see that when God is ready to move you out of what is no longer serving you, He will sometimes allow circumstances to do what your heart cannot. That move marked the beginning of something new for both Olivia and me.

Olivia's boyfriend at the time, Jorge, was instrumental in our move. He refused to let me spend money on professional movers. Instead, he took time off work and, almost single-handedly, helped us load the U-Haul. It was one of those quiet acts of service that speaks louder than words, strength offered without conditions.

The day after we arrived in Georgia, we were driving back from dropping Jorge at the airport when something holy unfolded in the car. Olivia was staring up at the sky when God began speaking to her heart. She later told me He said, "It's all going to be okay. Your life is about to change. You're right where you need to be." She was suddenly overwhelmed with love and peace, as if she were being watched over.

I was driving, but I could see her from the corner of my eye. She was beaming. I asked her what was going on, and she smiled and said, "You're not going to believe this. God told me not to tell you just yet."

I felt offended. If God was speaking, surely He would not exclude me. I thought I knew God better than she did. The truth, harder to admit, was that I was uncomfortable. Part of me wondered if she was hearing voices, and I looked at her strangely. While she radiated peace, I quietly slipped into fear.

After that short drive home, we went to our separate rooms to finish unpacking. But something had already shifted.

Over the next several months, Olivia fell deeply in love with Jesus through reading her Bible. She told me that God did not want her listening to podcasts or being influenced by other voices. He wanted to teach her Himself. Her faith was simple, pure, and unfiltered.

On a long drive to Tennessee to celebrate her twenty-second birthday, she tried to talk to me about Jesus. I responded from my own hardened heart and pride, defending my New Age beliefs and insisting that I knew Jesus better than she did. Scripture warns us, "Woe to those who are offended" (Isaiah 29:15–16), and looking back, I can see how offense had quietly hardened my heart.

Two months after that trip, Olivia invited me to church.

It was a church filled mostly with college-aged students. As I watched these young people, especially the young men, worship Jesus with their whole hearts, something inside me awakened. I remembered the deep love I once had for Christ. I remembered who I was before life, loss, and striving complicated my faith. Over the previous few years, I had been earnestly searching, but I was not in an atmosphere where I felt the Spirit of God moving. I explored other religions, yet being in that room with young hearts fully surrendered to the Lord gave me what I had been yearning for. That moment became the opening, my way back.

One month after this experience, I had a dream in which I believed God was telling me that an old childhood friend was my future husband. I spoke about this in an earlier chapter. Looking back, I now understand that the enemy knew what was unfolding in my life and was doing his best to derail me.

Olivia and I began regularly attending church and studying the Bible together, all initiated by Olivia. As the months went by, my awakening and love for God grew more intense. At the beginning of 2025, I entered into a fast, seeking clarity about whether David was meant to be my husband. While I did not receive an answer before we became engaged, the truth became clear just a few weeks after the engagement.

By April, it was evident that we were not aligned in important values. I ended the engagement, confused and deeply hurt. I questioned why God would allow me to walk through yet another painful ending. Had I not already been through enough? Yet instead of turning away from God, I pressed in. I needed to understand what was still unhealed within me that kept leading me into relationships that could not last.

In September, for her twenty-third birthday, Olivia wanted to travel to a deliverance ministry in Florida and be baptized. She had tried to be baptized at our local church, but the available spots filled within minutes. So on her birthday, we made the six-hour drive to Orlando, and the following day we were baptized together.

This was a deeply sacred moment for me. In 2023, it had been the desire of my heart for the three of us to be baptized together before Jourdan passed. While Jourdan was not with us in body, I was grateful that Olivia and I were able to share this moment together on such a meaningful occasion.

Olivia was baptized first, and it was prophesied over her that she would evangelize, lead her generation toward

Christ, and use her gift of singing as part of a worship team. I went next and received the prophecy that I was a prophet and a prayer warrior. While I had always sensed the gift of spiritual knowing, I had never considered myself a prophet. Still, I received the word in faith. Scripture says, "Believe the prophets, and you will prosper" (2 Chronicles 20:20).

After that, I began fasting again, and it took me even deeper into the things of God. Slowly, I became less interested in my old way of life. My appetites changed. My desires shifted.

This journey, my return to Jesus, is what brings me to this book.

I made a decision to wholeheartedly follow Christ, no matter the cost. No relationship, belief system, or coping mechanism was worth risking intimacy with Him. In His kindness, God began exposing and healing old patterns, especially my tendency to seek fulfillment, safety, or identity outside of Him.

As Scripture promises, "Seek first the kingdom of God and His righteousness, and all these things will be added to you" (Matthew 6:33).

This was not the end of the story. It was the beginning.

With every new beginning comes the surfacing of old wounds. As I returned to God, buried emotions, beliefs, and spiritual strongholds began to rise to the surface, not to shame me, but to be healed. In the next chapter, we will step into the process of healing and deliverance, where God lovingly confronts what has been hidden so freedom can fully take root.

JOURNAL PROMPTS

Take a moment to pause before moving forward. You do not need to have perfect answers. Simply notice what stirs in your heart.

1. How do you personally recognize the voice of God? What has it sounded or felt like in your life?
2. When was the last time God invited you into something new, even if it felt uncomfortable or unfamiliar?
3. Are there beliefs, practices, or attachments that once felt safe but may now be competing with intimacy with Christ?
4. What might God be gently asking you to release in order to follow Him more wholeheartedly?
5. Where do you sense God offering healing rather than correction in this season?

You may wish to journal, pray, or simply sit quietly with these questions before continuing.

HEALING OUR SOULS . HEALING OUR SOULS . HEALING OUR SOULS . HEALING OUR SOULS .

CHAPTER 11

And when ye stand praying, forgive, if ye have ought against any: that your Father also which is in heaven may forgive you your trespasses.

Mark 11:25

CHAPTER 11

UNDERSTANDING TRAUMA AND THE PATH OF HEALING

DISCLAIMER

This section is written from personal experience and faith-based practice. I am not a licensed therapist, counselor, or medical professional. Nothing in these pages is intended to diagnose, treat, cure, or prevent any medical or mental health condition. If you are experiencing a medical or mental health emergency, please call 911 or seek immediate professional help. Readers are encouraged to consult qualified physicians, therapists, or other licensed professionals, including faith-based providers if that aligns with your values, for medical, psychological, or psychiatric care. This book is meant to complement, not replace, professional support.

TRAUMA — WHAT IT IS AND HOW IT SHAPES US

This chapter is about understanding how wounds form, how doors open, and how, by God's grace, we can close them. This chapter becomes a bit more technical, but bear with me as I lay the foundation so that the healing process and steps will make more sense and be more effective.

Trauma is not defined solely by what happened to you. Trauma is defined by what happened inside of you as a result of what you experienced. Two people can live through the same event and walk away carrying very different internal wounds. Trauma forms when an experience overwhelms the nervous system's ability to process, cope, and return to a sense of safety.

Trauma can come from a single event such as abuse, loss, violence, an accident, or even witnessing a tragedy you were not directly involved in. Statistics show that approximately 70 percent of the world's population has been exposed to at least one traumatic life event. Trauma is part of the human experience. While exposure is high, only a portion of those exposed will go on to experience lasting symptoms such as PTSD, or Post Traumatic Stress Disorder.

In addition to what is often referred to as "Big T" trauma, trauma can also occur through what is known as "Little T" trauma. These are repeated experiences that may appear small on the surface but occur without relief, protection, or comfort, and over time can leave deep internal wounds. Chronic criticism, emotional neglect, instability, fear, abandonment, or living in a volatile environment can all shape the inner world of a child. Trauma is especially impactful when it occurs during the formative years of development, from birth through late adolescence, generally considered up to ages eighteen or nineteen.

During these years, the brain, nervous system, and sense of identity are still developing. Experiences are therefore absorbed more deeply and stored not just as memories, but as patterns of safety, belief, and expectation about the world. The most sensitive and high-risk period is early childhood, particularly from birth to age five.

This helps explain why siblings can be affected so differently by the same environment. A younger child's less developed brain and nervous system are more likely to register stress not only as a threat, but as a message about their worth and who they are. An older child may have more developed reasoning skills, a more established sense of self, or supportive connections with teachers, friends, or extended family that help soften the impact.

When trauma happens, the brain and body adapt for survival. The goal becomes safety, not growth. The nervous system learns to stay alert, scanning for danger, rejection, or abandonment. This state is often called hypervigilance. Over time, hypervigilance becomes a way of life. The mind races. Thoughts loop. Emotions feel overwhelming or shut down completely. Stillness can feel unsafe because the body has learned that danger often arrives when things are quiet. Resting or relaxing can feel threatening because the body expects the next shoe to drop. As a result, the nervous system becomes dysregulated.

A dysregulated nervous system does not know how to rest. Fight, flight, freeze, or fawn responses become automatic survival patterns. *Fight* can look like anger or control. *Flight* often appears as anxiety or constant busyness. *Freeze* may show up as shutdown, numbness, or feeling stuck. *Fawn*, or people-pleasing, looks like over-accommodating others to stay safe. These patterns can show up in different ways. Some stay busy and productive. Others withdraw or dissociate. Some swing between extremes. These responses are not character flaws. They are adaptations.

Trauma also shapes how we see God, ourselves, and other people. If love was inconsistent or conditional, we may believe we must perform to be accepted. If authority figures were unsafe, controlling, absent, or hypocritical, we may struggle to trust God's guidance, protection, or provision. We may find it difficult to see Him as a safe and loving Father, especially if the people who claimed to represent Him caused harm. If our emotions were ignored, punished, or mocked, we may learn to suppress them or feel shame for having them at all.

Scripture affirms that human beings are a three part being, spirit, soul, and body. "May your whole spirit, soul, and body be kept blameless at the coming of our Lord Jesus Christ" (1 Thessalonians 5:23). Trauma does not respect those boundaries. What affects the soul often shows up in the body. Fear, anxiety, chronic stress, autoimmune conditions, digestive issues, headaches, and fatigue are frequently connected to unresolved trauma. Scripture affirms this connection. "A joyful heart is good medicine, but a crushed spirit dries up the bones" (Proverbs 17:22).

My sister Joan was diagnosed with Multiple Sclerosis around the age of eighteen or nineteen. She lived with the disease for over four decades before learning information that reframed her understanding of her symptoms. After moving from Las Vegas to Tennessee, her new specialist wanted to better understand seizures she had previously experienced. She was connected to an electroencephalogram (EEG) to record brain activity during a medically induced seizure. Interestingly, the seizure did not register on the machine. She was told that the type of seizures she experienced would not respond to medication. She was then referred to a psychologist who explored her childhood history.

Ultimately, the doctors concluded that her seizures were trauma induced and rooted in unresolved childhood experiences. The recommended course of treatment was counseling rather than medication.

Modern research echoes what Scripture has long revealed. The body keeps a record of experiences even when the mind tries to move on. This reality is explored in depth in *The Body Keeps the Score* by Dr. Bessel van der Kolk.

Many people misunderstand trauma because they associate it only with extreme events. They tell themselves things like others had it worse, that was normal, or I should be over this by now. Trauma is not about comparison. It is about impact. What overwhelms one person may not overwhelm another, but the nervous system does not lie.

Trauma can also fracture identity. When a child or adult is overwhelmed and unsupported, parts of the soul learn to retreat in order to survive. This can create a sense of fragmentation, as though pieces of the self were left behind in moments that were too painful to endure. The Bible describes this impact as crushed and shattered. Scripture often uses the image of a broken vessel to describe the soul after trauma. In Psalm 31:12, David says, *"I have become like broken pottery."* This helps explain why many people feel disconnected from their true selves, unsure of who they are apart from the roles they play, the responsibilities they carry, and the coping strategies they have adopted.

I remember sitting alone on the grass as a child, quietly repeating the words, "I am me." Even then, I sensed there was something deeper inside of me than what the outside world reflected. Somewhere along the way, that knowing was lost. Like many trauma survivors, I spent much of my life trying to find my way back to myself.

Trauma does not just shape behavior. It shapes beliefs. It teaches the brain what to expect from life. If danger was frequent, the brain expects danger. If love was unpredictable, the heart stays guarded. If joy was followed by loss, the body learns to brace against anticipated doom, even in good moments.

Trauma explains many things that once felt confusing or condemning. It helps us understand why rest can feel uncomfortable, why joy may feel unfamiliar, why the mind replays the past, and why fear can feel ever present.

Trauma can also be inherited. Some of the pain people carry did not begin with them. It began with their parents, grandparents, or generations before them. Scripture acknowledges this reality while also pointing toward redemption. "The sins of the parents are visited upon the children" is a pattern described in Scripture, but so is the promise that God shows steadfast love to a thousand generations of those who love Him (Exodus 20:5–6).

A modern psychological exploration of this pattern can be found in *It Didn't Start With You* by Mark Wolynn, which examines how unresolved trauma can be passed down through family systems and even biological stress responses.

Research supports this reality. Studies of Holocaust survivors and their descendants have shown that trauma can alter stress responses across generations. Children and grandchildren of survivors often exhibit heightened anxiety and altered cortisol levels, even when they did not experience the original trauma themselves. Similar patterns are being explored among descendants of enslaved Africans, where chronic fear, loss, and survival stress were not only learned behaviorally but also carried within the body's stress response systems.

We readily accept that illnesses such as cancer or heart disease can be inherited. Yet we are slower to acknowledge that trauma, addiction patterns, emotional dysregulation, and chronic stress responses can also be passed down. Addiction, for example, is shaped both by environment and by biological vulnerability influenced by generational stress. Recognizing inherited trauma is not about blame. It is about clarity.

Understanding trauma does not excuse sin, but it does cultivate compassion. From that place, real healing can begin. Scripture defines sin using the Greek word *hamartia*, meaning to miss the mark. In this light, sin is less about condemnation and more about deviation from what brings life, safety, and wholeness. God's opposition to sin is rooted in love, because sin is destructive, deceptive, and ultimately separates people from the communion and freedom He desires for them. His guidance is not meant to control us, but to protect, restore, and lead us into a more abundant life.

Inviting God into these places can look very practical:

1. pausing
2. asking God a question
3. sitting with Him in discomfort
4. noticing what rises in your body or thoughts
5. surrendering an outcome
6. obeying a quiet instruction

Scripture assures us that God does not shame us for our wounds. "The Lord is near to the brokenhearted and saves those who are crushed in spirit" (Psalm 34:18). He does not rush the process. He restores. "He heals the brokenhearted and binds up their wounds" (Psalm 147:3).

This is why healing is not simply about changing thoughts. Healing requires safety. The nervous system must learn that the threat has passed. This happens gradually as awareness grows, as truth replaces old conclusions, and as the body is given repeated experiences of safety. Healing unfolds as we understand what happened, learn to respond differently in the present, practice new patterns over time, and intentionally invite God into the places that once felt overwhelming or unsafe.

God reveals so that He can heal. Awareness is not the end goal. Restoration is.

JOURNAL PROMPTS

Take a few quiet moments to reflect. You may want to write, pray, or simply notice what comes up.

1. As you think about your childhood or family history, what wounds or patterns do you recognize that may have been passed down from previous generations? If you notice similar patterns showing up in two or three family members, this could indicate a generational or bloodline influence.

2. How have these wounds shown up in your body, your relationships, or your beliefs about yourself or God?

3. What coping strategies did you develop to survive, even if they no longer serve you today?

4. Where do you sense God inviting you into greater safety, self-care, and compassion toward yourself?

If at any point this reflection feels overwhelming, you are not required to push through. You may set it aside and return to it later, or choose to process it with a trusted counselor, pastor, or trauma-informed professional. Healing is not rushed, and you are not alone in it.

THE HEALING OUR SOULS METHOD™ EXPLAINED

A Gentle, Repeatable Guide for Working Through Trauma, Pain, and Emotional Triggers

Now that we've covered some of the heavier material, let's look at how we can find relief from these wounds. Healing happens when truth is allowed to move through the body, not just the mind. Trauma and emotional pain are not stored only in our thoughts; they are held in the nervous system, the body, and the soul, including the mind, will, and emotions.

Spiritually, healing begins when false beliefs are brought into the light, forgiveness is extended, repentance brings our hearts back into agreement with God's truth, and Jesus is invited into the places where pain and fragmentation first occurred. This is central to His ministry. Jesus did not only forgive sins. He healed bodies, restored minds, and made the brokenhearted whole.

WHY NAMING EMOTIONS MATTERS

Naming what you feel is one of the most important steps in healing. In Scripture, when Jesus encountered the demonized man, He asked a simple question: "What is your name?" The response was "Legion." Jesus did not ask because He lacked authority; He asked so that what was hidden could be exposed. It is worth repeating that what is revealed can be healed.

When you name fear, grief, shame, abandonment, addiction, or any other emotion or issue, you take it out of hiding. This brings both spiritual clarity and internal calm. Many people were never taught how to name what they feel, and this process gently restores that ability.

WHAT IS HAPPENING IN THE BODY

Your body is designed to protect you. When something feels threatening, even emotionally, your nervous system responds automatically. This is why you may feel your heart racing, tightness in your chest, or tingling sensations in your fingers, toes, or other extremities when you are triggered.

For many years, I felt tingling in my body during emotional moments and had no idea what it was. It was just a few years ago when I learned that my body was responding before my mind could make sense of it. If you experience this or similar sensations, know that your body is not malfunctioning. It is communicating.

These sensations often occur because the nervous system releases stress chemicals, such as adrenaline, when the body senses danger, even emotional danger. This is part of the fight, flight, freeze, fawn response. As safety returns, those chemicals begin to settle, and the body starts to release stored tension, fear, and emotional stress that were never given a way to resolve.

The body will often settle once it no longer senses danger in the moment. Breathing, distraction, or calming activities can bring temporary relief. But if the underlying trigger is not healed, the sensations and emotional reactions will return.

This is why many people turn to things like food, alcohol, smoking, overworking, or staying busy to feel better. These may help for a moment, but they do not resolve what the body and soul are holding. The nervous system will continue to react until the root issue is addressed. Healing is important because it brings lasting change, not just temporary relief.

I share this method because I lived this cycle for decades without understanding what was happening. I do not want others to spend years managing symptoms when wholeness is available. This method helped me experience real breakthroughs by addressing the root, not just the reaction.

WHY THIS METHOD IS GENTLE AND EFFECTIVE

This method works because it does not force healing. It creates safety for healing to unfold. It brings awareness instead of avoidance. It restores choice where fear once ruled. It invites truth into places shaped by pain and where lies were once believed. It allows the body to release emotional stress that was never given permission to resolve.

If you are having difficulty identifying what you are feeling or what needs healing, pray about it. You can simply say, God, please show me the area in my life where I am ready for healing and what emotions and situation is connected to this. The quality of your life is based on the quality of the questions you ask God and what you do with those answers. So, ask God for clarity often, then act on what He reveals.

God is faithful to reveal truth in love and in the right timing.

FORGIVENESS AND REPENTANCE

Forgiveness and repentance are both vital to healing, but they serve different purposes. Forgiveness releases the burden of anger, resentment, or hurt caused by others. It does not mean condoning what happened or allowing harmful patterns to continue. Repentance is about acknowledging our own missteps, making amends when necessary, turning away from the behavior, and realigning our hearts with God's. Together, they break cycles of emotional, spiritual, and even physical stress, opening space for restoration and peace. Scripture reminds us, "Forgive as the Lord forgave you" (Colossians 3:13), and repentance is woven throughout Scripture as a path to renewal and alignment with God's will (Acts 3:19).

THE BEAUTY OF FORGIVENESS

In my own life, I have seen the beauty of forgiveness. Many years before I knew my sister's support would be critical in my life, Angela came to me with a sincere apology for things that had happened long before. By that time, I was no longer carrying resentment toward her, even before the apology came. I often reflect on what might have been lost had I held onto bitterness instead.

When I did not have the strength to face certain realities, Angela stepped in with quiet courage and compassion. She carried burdens I could not carry at the time, and her presence reminded me that forgiveness opens the door to unexpected grace. God often uses others to bring healing, support, and wisdom precisely when we need it most.

Angela has always shown generosity toward my children, continuing to love and support them in tangible ways, even as they grew into adulthood. Her faithfulness over the years has shown me that forgiveness does not only free the heart. It creates space for life giving relationships to grow.

You never know who God will use to support you in a later season. I deeply treasure the relationship Angela, and I have shared over the years, one that has grown beyond past wounds into a beautiful, mutually supportive bond.

THE CONSEQUENCES OF UNFORGIVENESS

I have also seen the other side of unforgiveness. When unforgiveness takes root, you can become the very thing you hate or grow bitter and hardened. Unforgiveness is like a cancer. It quietly eats away at the heart. When you forgive, you are not excusing the act. You are freeing yourself from what was done to you.

I have seen lives destroyed when unforgiveness and bitterness are allowed to take root. You may ask, "Why should I forgive them for what they did to me?" I ask you to consider why God forgives us again and again for the hurtful and destructive things we do.

If you are still seething with anger over something that happened in the past, it is likely that unforgiveness is still operating. If you want to stop hurting, you can take a first step by praying something simple, such as, "Father God, please give me the strength to be open to forgiving (name) for what they have done to me." Say this prayer as often as needed until something begins to shift.

As the anger softens over time, you may be able to go deeper and say, "Father, I forgive (name) for what they did to me." You will know healing has taken place when you can see, think about, or hear the person's name without anger rising up. You are no longer blaming them for ruining your life, and you accept that we are all imperfect people trying to find our way.

Forgiveness does not require continued contact. I am not suggesting you remain in relationship with someone who has not changed or whose presence is harmful to your physical or mental health. Forgiveness can also be done for those who have passed away. Their death does not resolve what happened or how you feel unless you choose to resolve it within yourself.

BIBLICAL EXAMPLES

In the book of 2 Samuel, Tamar was raped by her half-brother Amnon, the son of King David. After assaulting her, Amnon rejected her and sent her away, leaving her in shame and devastation. When Tamar's full brother Absalom learned what had happened, he was consumed with anger. He waited two years and then had Amnon killed. King David mourned Amnon, but Scripture does not record that he brought justice or addressed the deeper wound. Over time, David's unresolved grief and anger toward Absalom and lack of reconciliation contributed to further division. Eventually, Absalom was killed by Joab, David's general. Other than Tamar, scripture does not show that anyone confessed, repented, or sought forgiveness. Four lives were deeply damaged because unforgiveness and silence were allowed to fester after one act of violence.

Another example is found in the book of Esther. Haman harbored deep hatred toward Mordecai, a Jewish man who refused to dishonor God by bowing to him. Haman's bitterness grew until he issued a decree to destroy Mordecai and all the Jewish people. When Haman later learned that Mordecai had once saved the king's life, he had an opportunity to humble himself and release his hatred. Instead, pride blinded him. Haman and his ten sons were ultimately executed, while Mordecai was honored, promoted, and celebrated throughout the kingdom.

These stories remind us that unforgiveness does not remain contained. It spreads, destroys, and multiplies pain. Forgiveness, though difficult, interrupts that cycle and creates space for healing, truth, and freedom.

SHAME

I was forgiven. I was saved. But I had no framework for understanding that salvation of the spirit does not automatically retrain the nervous system. Trauma can remain buried for years. Mine did not begin to fully surface until 2011, when I was triggered by the trauma of a pulmonary embolism. What had been quietly stored in my body rose to the surface under stress. It had not disappeared. It had simply been dormant.

That does not mean Jesus failed to heal me. It means healing is often progressive and experiential. Redemption is immediate. Restoration of the mind and nervous system takes time.

Trauma like fear, shame, and guilt carves deep neural pathways in the brain. These pathways become efficient and automatic.

When we begin healing work through prayer, therapy, or intentional reflection such as journaling, we are building new neural pathways. At first, they are weak and unfamiliar. The brain defaults to the old pathway because it is established and energy efficient.

The new pathway requires repetition, awareness, and intentional choice. Over time, as safe responses are practiced consistently, the new pathway becomes stronger and more accessible.

Fear and shame were the deepest threads woven through my story.

My earliest memory of shame goes back to when I was about four years old. My best friend Phillip and I were playing under a table when my mother caught what she believed was inappropriate behavior. I do not remember the details clearly. We were children. I only remember her yelling and the sudden wave of humiliation that flooded my body.

I was four years old. I did not have language for what was happening, but something settled inside me that day.

Shame attached itself to that moment.

It followed me into other experiences.

I felt shame when Mr. Morgan touched me inappropriately. I felt shame when men catcalled me on the streets of New York. I felt shame growing up poor. I felt shame not being raised in a two-parent household. I felt shame about the division in my family. I felt shame about being divorced twice and becoming a single mother. I felt shame when my son died, not because I believed I had failed him, but because I feared others might see me as a failure as a mother. I felt shame that my life did not unfold the way I expected.

Shame is rarely satisfied with one incident. Once it finds a place to anchor, it looks for evidence to reinforce itself. Every painful event becomes confirmation of the same lie: Something is wrong with you.

I did therapy. I journaled. I prayed. Yet a part of my soul still felt stuck in that early memory. It had been there for over fifty years.

When I invited Jesus into that scene and asked Him to comfort me under that table and lead me to safety, I felt the greatest shift. I did not try to rewrite what happened. I asked Him to step into the place where I had felt exposed and confused. I asked Him to speak truth over the four-year-old version of me. I asked Him to restore what shame had shattered.

Healing did not happen in a single moment. It unfolded as I repeatedly returned to Him, choosing truth and safety over the old narrative that said, I am a bad girl.

JESUS THE HEALER

Jesus does not only forgive sin. He heals wounds. He is fully God and fully man. He knows rejection, betrayal, grief, and physical suffering. He wept at the tomb of Lazarus. In the Garden of Gethsemane, He felt deep anguish as He anticipated betrayal by Judas, abandonment by Peter, and death on the cross. He understands emotional pain from the inside.

Throughout the Gospels, we see Him restoring more than bodies.

In John 8:1–11, religious leaders brought a woman caught in adultery and placed her before Him publicly. She stood exposed, condemned, and humiliated. Jesus did not participate in her shaming. He confronted her accusers, then addressed her directly. "Neither do I condemn you. Go and sin no more." He protected her dignity before correcting her behavior. Shame was not His tool.

He proclaimed that He came to heal the brokenhearted and set the oppressed free.

And with Peter, we see something deliberate and precise. On the night of Jesus' arrest, Peter denied Him three times. When the rooster crowed, Peter remembered Jesus' words and wept bitterly. Luke 22:54–62 records Peter's denial, and John 18:18 notes that he was standing by a charcoal fire when it happened.

After the resurrection, in John 21:9–17, Jesus met the disciples by the Sea of Galilee. John again notes a charcoal fire. Breakfast was prepared.

Three times Jesus asked Peter, *"Do you love Me?"*

Three times Peter answered.

And three times Jesus said, *"Feed My sheep."*

The location was different. The failure was not erased. But Jesus addressed it directly. He did not reduce Peter to his denial. He restored him and entrusted him with leadership over His people.

Jesus heals at the level of identity. He addresses the false conclusions we formed about ourselves in moments of fear and shame.

Now that we've laid a solid foundation, let's look at the Healing Our Souls Method™.

IMPORTANT NOTE

The Healing Our Souls Method™ can be used alongside professional and spiritual care when needed. I think of it like this. Counseling, therapy, and spiritual support are like deep care that addresses long-standing issues over time. This method is something you can use in everyday moments, when emotions surface.

It does not replace deeper work. What it does is give you something practical to use in the moment when feelings come up, instead of pushing them aside.

Healing happens layer by layer, not all at once. You wouldn't expect to build muscle from a single trip to the gym. You keep showing up until you see the results you want. This method works the same way. Keep using it until the wound no longer unsettles you.

HOW DO YOU KNOW HEALING IS NEEDED? (SELF-CHECK)

Consider the following questions prayerfully:

1. Do you feel emotionally reactive or overwhelmed?
2. Do you experience persistent sadness, numbness, or anxiety?
3. Are you frequently angry, irritable, or easily triggered?
4. Do you cry easily without knowing why, or struggle to connect with your emotions at all?
5. Are you avoiding people, places, or memories?
6. Do you carry shame or guilt that feels unresolved?

7. Do you feel unsettled even when life is going well?
8. Have these feelings lasted more than a few days or weeks?

If you identify with several of these, healing work may be needed. Let's get started.

WHAT YOU WILL NEED

- Your journal or something to write on
- A pen
- Your Bible, if you want to look up scripture
- A quiet space
- A glass of water, optional but encouraged

THE HEALING OUR SOULS METHOD™

STEP 1: NOTICE

What to Do

Pause when you feel triggered.

What it Looks Like

A racing heart, shallow breathing, trembling, muscle tension, sweating, or chills. You may also notice anger, withdrawal, avoidance, excuses, or dishonesty.

STEP 2: NAME

What to Do

Name the emotion you are feeling and where you feel it in your body.

What it Looks Like

I *feel* afraid. My *heart* is racing and I have butterflies in my stomach.

STEP 3: ALLOW

What to Do

Sit with the emotion. Do not rush to fix it.

What it Looks Like

I pause and allow myself to feel the discomfort instead of distracting myself or pushing it away.

STEP 4: ASK

What to Do

Ask what this feeling is connected to and where you have felt it before. Pray for insight. Journaling may also help to uncover the root.

What it Looks Like

Father God, please reveal what this fear is connected to and where it began.

STEP 5: ACKNOWLEDGE

What to Do

Say out loud what you have discovered about what you are experiencing.

What it Looks Like

I feel afraid that Maria will be upset with me if I do not go along with her plans.

STEP 6: FORGIVE OTHERS / FORGIVE YOURSELF

What to Do

Forgive those who contributed to the wound or pattern, ask for forgiveness for ways you may have hurt others or repeated similar patterns.

What it Looks Like (Forgive Others)

I forgive my parents and siblings for creating a hostile home environment and making me feel responsible for being the "good one".

What it Looks Like (Forgive Yourself)

Father, please forgive me for secretly resenting my parents and siblings and blaming all my problems on them.

STEP 7: REPENT AND REPLACE

What to Do

Repent for believing a lie that formed from the hurt. Come out of agreement with it and replace it with God's truth.

What it Looks Like

I repent for believing the lie that my value comes from being useful, that I am responsible for making sure everyone is okay, and that the disappointment of others means I have failed.

I come out of agreement with these lies.

The truth is my worth was established by God at creation. I am fearfully and wonderfully made. Real love is not a trade.

There is no fear in love, but perfect love drives out fear. I am not the savior. I am allowed to have boundaries.

STEP 8: INVITE

What to Do

Invite Jesus to heal the wounded places in your soul.

What it Looks Like

Jesus, I invite You into my heart. Heal the places where I am still holding pain from (incident).

Heal the (emotion) in my body and the belief that (false belief from Step 7)

Example: love had to be earned by being good.

Heal my memories from this incident and restore them with truth, compassion, and Your peace.

STEP 9: RELEASE

What to Do

Slowly breathe in God's peace. Exhale and release the pain you've been carrying.

What it Looks Like

Breathe in the *Ruach*, the life-giving breath of God, and breathe out allowing your body to relax and know that the danger has passed.

STEP 10: GIVE THANKS

What to Do

Thank God for the healing you have received, even if it feels subtle or incomplete. Acknowledge His presence, care, and faithfulness in the method.

What it Looks Like

Jesus, thank You for meeting me in this place.

Thank You for the healing You have begun in my heart, body, and memories.

I receive Your truth, Your peace, and Your love, and I trust You to continue the work You have started in Me.

What Release May Look Like in the Body

You may experience:

- Deep sighing or repeated breaths
- Crying
- Yawning
- Burping
- Passing gas
- A sense of warmth or relaxation
- Feeling tired and needing to take a nap
- Feeling lighter like a burden has been lifted

Let it happen. Do not analyze it. Your body knows how to let go.

AFTERCARE AND ONGOING HEALING

- Drink water after the method. Prayer refreshes the spirit. Water refreshes the body.
- Write down anything that came up for you.
- If something new arises, either work through it using the same steps or make a note to return to it later.
- Repeat this method as often as needed.
- Healing happens in layers. It does not happen all at once.

A GENTLE REMINDER FOR THE READER

You are not doing this wrong. This method is fluid. You can mix the steps, adjust them, and make them your own. Trust yourself. Your heart and soul know what to say. You are not weak for needing to return to this work again and again. Healing is not about fixing yourself. It is about coming back to your whole self, the person you were always meant to be. It is about coming back into truth, safety, and love. God is patient. Your soul is wise. Take your time.

THE HEALING OUR SOULS METHOD™ WHEEL

Here is a wheel that graphically shows the steps. You may want to take a picture of it so you can have it with you whenever you need it.

FINAL REFLECTION

The most healing realization for me has been this: telling my story has set me free. For years, parts of my life felt like something to hide, explain, or soften. Writing this book changed that. I am no longer hiding in the shadows. I am no longer shrinking. If you have ever felt the need to shrink and hide, I hope you are beginning to see that you do not have to.

Telling my story has removed the weight of shame I carried for too long. I am not the only person who has walked through complicated family dynamics. I am not the only person who has made mistakes. I am not the only parent whose children have struggled. I am not the only mother who has lost a child.

And you are not the only one either. Pain is not proof of failure. It is proof that we have lived. Shame loses its power when it is brought into the light.

There were moments when I felt misunderstood or judged. Some of that came from others' unresolved pain. I understand that now. I no longer carry responsibility for how others choose to see me. You are not responsible for carrying that weight either.

I am learning to accept what God sees in me and what He says about me. I am wise. I am fearfully and wonderfully made. I am kind and discerning. These qualities are strengths, not liabilities. And if you belong to Him, those same truths apply to you. As I have walked through this life, I have experienced real pain. Now I choose to embrace joy and growth. In many ways, I see myself in the story of Joseph. What the enemy meant for harm, God used for good. What the enemy hoped would keep me quiet became the platform for my voice. I was not meant to keep silent. I was meant to speak and declare the goodness of God.

And now I do.

If this book has stirred something in you, perhaps you were not meant to stay silent either. Perhaps your story, too, is meant to bring healing. Perhaps what once felt like shame is actually the very place where God will reveal His restoration.

HEALING OUR SOULS · HEALING OUR SOULS · HEALING OUR SOULS · HEALING OUR SOULS ·

CLOSING

If ye be willing and obedient, ye shall eat the good of the land.

Isaiah 1:19

CLOSING

I have been crucified with Christ. It is no longer I who live, but Christ who lives in me. And the life I now live in the flesh I live by faith in the Son of God, who loved me and gave Himself for me. — Galatians 2:20. I hope you have found this book helpful and encouraging as you continue your healing journey.

I still have areas where I am growing and healing. Two of my current focus areas are deepening my confidence in what God has called me to do and fully partnering with Him and building consistency in carrying out what He has entrusted to me. Writing this book is a major step in that direction. I am now a finisher of a significant assignment.

If you have reached the end of this book, I want to honor you. It takes courage to stay present and open through difficult truths. That means you are a finisher too. I celebrate you, and I celebrate what God is doing in both of us. Where God will take me next, I do not know. But I will ask you this: What is the last thing God asked you to do? Have you done it?

If along this journey you sensed a deeper pull, a longing for God, or a quiet knowing that you want to give your life to Him or return to Him with an open heart, I invite you to pray the Prayer of Salvation found earlier in this book. Read it slowly. Say it sincerely. God meets us exactly where we are, and He honors a willing heart.

CLOSING PRAYER

This is my prayer for you.

Father God,

Thank You for the work You have begun in this heart. Thank You for meeting them right where they are, with compassion, mercy, and truth. Continue to heal what has been wounded, restore what has been broken, and strengthen what is being rebuilt. Fill them with Your peace, Your presence, and Your love. Lead them forward in wisdom, courage, and faith. May they come to know You more deeply, trust You more fully, and walk in the freedom You desire for them.

Your Word says that He who began a good work in us will carry it on to completion until the day of Christ Jesus. We stand on that promise.

In Jesus' Name. Amen.

If you prayed the Prayer of Salvation and gave your life to God, I would love to celebrate with you. Please feel free to email me at support@healingoursouls.com and let me know. It would be an honor to rejoice with you in this new beginning.

If you do not have a church home, I encourage you to seek out a place where you can grow, be supported, and fellowship with other believers. We were not meant to walk this journey alone. Scripture reminds us not to forsake gathering together, but to encourage one another as we grow in faith and love.

Healing does not end here. This is not a conclusion, but a continuation. Walk forward knowing that God is with you, for you, and faithful to complete the work He has begun.

Walking with you on your healing journey,

Pamela Marjorie

HealingOurSouls.com

Restoring what trauma stole

REFERENCES

- Crane, Dan. *Christ Over Culture: A Gospel Journey to Racial Redemption.*
- Prince, Derek. *Fasting: The Key to Releasing God's Power in Your Life.*
- Wolynn, Mark. *It Didn't Start With You: How Inherited Family Trauma Shapes Who We Are and How to End the Cycle.*
- van der Kolk, Bessel. *The Body Keeps the Score.*
- Montgomery, Tiphani. *The Year of the Bride Fast.* YouTube Videos, Day 1–25, August 4, 2025 – August 28, 2025.

CALL TO ACTION!

This Is More Than a Book. This Is a Movement. We are on a mission to reach 1,000,000 souls through:

- Salvation through Jesus Christ
- Lives re-dedicated to Christ
- Healing from emotional, childhood, and generational trauma

GET INVOLVED

Follow • Share • Be part of the healing

Instagram: @HOSwithPamelaMarjorie

STAY CONNECTED & GO DEEPER

Stay connected, receive ongoing encouragement, and explore ways to continue your healing journey. If you feel called to deeper, personal healing, you can learn more about private coaching sessions.

Visit: HealingOurSouls.com

TAKE YOUR PLACE IN THE MOVEMENT

You are not here by accident. What God is doing in your life is part of something bigger. Let's restore together what trauma tried to steal.